LATRE' MEDLEY

OnlyBandz

How To Become A Pornstar

First published by Midnite Dakota Publishing 2024

Copyright © 2024 by LaTre' Medley

All rights reserved. No part of this publication may be reproduced, stored or transmitted in any form or by any means, electronic, mechanical, photocopying, recording, scanning, or otherwise without written permission from the publisher. It is illegal to copy this book, post it to a website, or distribute it by any other means without permission.

LaTre' Medley asserts the moral right to be identified as the author of this work.

LaTre' Medley has no responsibility for the persistence or accuracy of URLs for external or third-party Internet Websites referred to in this publication and does not guarantee that any content on such Websites is, or will remain, accurate or appropriate.

Designations used by companies to distinguish their products are often claimed as trademarks. All brand names and product names used in this book and on its cover are trade names, service marks, trademarks and registered trademarks of their respective owners. The publishers and the book are not associated with any product or vendor mentioned in this book. None of the companies referenced within the book have endorsed the book.

The information provided in this book is for educational purposes only and is not intended as professional advice.

Cover design by LaTre' Medley

First edition

ISBN: 979-8-9915180-0-0

This book was professionally typeset on Reedsy. Find out more at reedsy.com

This Book Is Dedicated To All The Fake Friends That Revealed Themselves At A Time When I Needed You The Most! Without You, There Would Be No Me. Now I'm Bout To Spank Shit!

Contents

Acknowledgments	ii
I Love Love!	1
Understanding the Industry	10
Ask Yourself This	20
In The Beginning…	27
Making This Shit Last	35
Be Smart	43
If Your Gonna Do It, Then Do It	52
Who The Fuck Are You?	57
Get Dat Bread Get Dat Head With Onlyfans	65
Get Paid From Pornhub	69
Enhancements and Sexual Health	73
Secrets to Success	88
ACC vs Pornstar	94
Solo Scenes	99
Couple Content	110
Put Yourself Out There	114
First 24	119
Conclusion	124
Bibliography	128
Glossary	133
Support Services	147
Recommended Readings and Documentaries	148
About the Author	149

Acknowledgments

First and foremost, I want to extend my deepest gratitude to Jesscoyia Kline aka TOAO Jayne Doee. Your unwavering support, encouragement, and belief in me throughout this journey have been invaluable. Your insights and guidance have helped shape this book, and for that, I am forever grateful.

A special thank you to Ashton Younger for your incredible support and contributions. Your friendship, feedback, and patience have been instrumental in bringing this book to life. I couldn't have done it without your help.

I would like to extend my heartfelt gratitude to the individuals whose pioneering work made this book possible. In particular, Ilya Sutskever's groundbreaking contributions have been instrumental in shaping the tools and technologies that underpin this project. Your influence is deeply appreciated and has made a lasting impact on the field. To everyone who played a role, big or small, in the creation of this book, thank you. Your support means the world to me.

Also… Fuck James "Jamie" Wilson.

I Love Love!

So, ya think you got what it takes to be in the Adult Industry? We shall see about that my friend! We are going to be covering a wide range of topics in this book, but before we get started, it's probably a good idea if I tell you a little bit about myself. Hi, my name is LaTre' and I love love, and always have! I'm not sure how you'll feel about this next statement, but I legit "get off" on the thought of being a provider. I love the concept of a happy family life and taking care of the woman I'm in love with. Unfortunately, that concept has been strongly misguided. I was missing a very important piece of the puzzle when it came to my idea of being a provider. It's just slightly important that the woman you love and are providing for, also loves you back. Well, who knew…

I clearly didn't get the memo because I decided to spend 1 year and 5 months being the best man I have ever been to any woman in my past to my girlfriend at the time, Dionna Hall. Dionna was beautiful! I would brag about her beauty to other people constantly. I was proud to have her by my side. She made me look good! She had beautiful soft skin like honey butter, curly hair that bounced when she walked, eyes like candy, and a cute birthmark right on her cheek that I spent most of our relationship kissing.

I took care of her the best way I could. I went above and beyond on every occasion just because I wanted her to give me just an ounce of the love back that I gave to her. I did everything for her. She ain't want for nothing and if she did I would do my best to get it. I paid her rent. Took care of her car. Spent thousands of dollars on Christmas presents for her and her family. Took care of her little sister when she couldn't afford to. Got her family from all across the United States into one building for her birthday, and paid for flights and vacations! Shit, my first 30 days of knowing her I took her to Las Vegas for Valentine's Day, I had met her on January 10, and On February 12th we were on a flight to Nevada for a week. Wrote songs for her and about her, and put her eyes on my album cover. Used the vocals of her deceased nephew to create a song their entire family could listen to in memory of him. All I wanted back was love and appreciation. Silly me…

Dionna was different, Dionna is what we refer to in the world today as an ungrateful… or heartless… or a Bitch… Oh, I got it! She's an Ungrateful Heartless Bitch! Flows right off the tongue doesn't it? The funny thing is she used to blame me for my own feelings. She said she told me how she was when we first met. Truth be told she was kinda right. When we first met we asked each other what our "Red Flags" were. I said something like "I keep picking the wrong women to love, I love too hard, and I stay even when I know I should go because I believe in working things out".

Dionna said "I have anger issues, and difficulties showing compassion. There will be a time when you're gonna be crying, pouring your heart out to me, and I will look you dead in your face and not give a single fuck". Then she finished her sentence off by saying "It's something I'm working on". Looking back at it now I should have ran while I had the chance, but stupid me ignored all of that, as if I didn't just hear the qualities that make up a serial killer.

Anyways, the relationship with her is a story within itself. I'll make sure to tell you soon! Let's fast forward to me finally being done with the ungrateful heartless bitch. We've officially broken up and I've moved into my new apartment, bought a new truck, got a dope new job, and a crazy new side hustle. On top of that, I've got something I've never had before in my entire life, a six-pack! I know what you're thinking, "you must have been working out". Nope, not at all! Just been crying, a lot. In fact, I spent most of that relationship in tears. I honestly didn't realize I was depressed. I also didn't really believe in depression until it happened to me. I lost so much weight. I was skin and bone, but the six-pack...it was there. Now it was time to turn it into something! Now that I'm out of the relationship I'm telling myself I'm going to stay single for a while.

From the age of 20 up until 30 I was never single for more than 2 or 3 months at a time. So being single was new to me. I had also just lost my grandfather around that time, so I'm really trying to figure some shit out about myself. By this point, I actually have started working out now. I lost all this weight from depression and I was scared I was going to fuck it up by getting happy again! So the gym was the solution. I was working really hard to tone my body. I loved the results I was getting.

At some point, I contacted a man by the name of James Wilson aka Jamie. I've been friends with him on Facebook for years but we only talked off and on, you know how this Facebook shit goes. I honestly don't know half the people I'm friends with up there and don't even remember sending or accepting all these damn people! I honestly don't even recall how I knew Jamie, I definitely had never seen him in person before, but we had a lot of mutual friends so I never dug too deep into it. Plus he was friends with people I trusted. I also could see by his profile that he was a successful real estate agent, and with my newfound singleness, I felt now was as perfect a time as any to pursue a goal.

I reached out to Jamie via Facebook Messenger and told him I wanted to be a real estate agent and that I was ready to take it seriously. I asked him to help me get started! I lied to you not, this man's exact response was "Ummm... Fuck That! Come Be A Hoe With Us!" Theirs just silence on my end.. I'm staring at the message confused as hell. So I said back to him "I don't understand. What do you mean? Like, with the other real estate agents? He said, "Lol, no, I'll show you." A few seconds later he sent me 3 or 4 videos of people having sex with a black staircase in the background. He told me that was his house. He also sent me his Instagram. I was baffled! My eyes are as big as an owl at this point! I see his Instagram and I'm flabbergasted.

Jamie owns an Adult Entertainment Talent Agency, while I'm finding all this information out my only thoughts are, "This is beyonnnddd me!" He made me an offer to come to a paint-and-sip party. He told me he would give me $200 just to come and bartend. Sounds like easy money to me so I agreed. Well, I get to the venue, that's not a venue, it's someone's basement. It's decorated nicely though. I'm looking at the walls and it's gotta be a good 2000 signatures on the wall, I'm intrigued. About 20 minutes into the event that I'm so-called "Bartending", which is basically handing out shots of Casimgo's or Hennessey, you know, black people shit! Jamie walks up to me with this weird look on his face. I thought I was doing something wrong, so I asked him what was up.

I lie to you not, this man Jamie said to me with a straight face… "Why is your shirt still on?" I paused for a second, honestly, I was a little taken aback by the question, it was definitely not expected. I say back to him "Ughhh because that's where it's supposed to be, this is a nice shirt, I got it from Ross!" Jamie then proceeded to roll his gay ass eyes at me and says "Listen to me, take your shirt off while you're handing out these shots and if any of these women ask if you have a OnlyFans or if you make content you tell them yes!" My eyes are huge like an owl again, tryna process what this man is telling me. I said to him "But Jamie, I don't have a OnlyFans and I don't make content". He says " Yes, yes you do". We went back and forth for about 20 seconds before Jamie finally said "Look you're starting to piss me off, just tell them yes". At this point I say screw it. I took the two shots I was holding right in front of him and said "Fine".

So as I'm handing out these shots, more women are coming into the event. They're all walking straight up to me asking the same questions. I do what Jamie tells me and I'm baffled! 8,9,10,11 Women back to back all with the exact same response "Oh My God you do OnlyFans, me too we need to work together". My eyes are once again as big as an Owl.

Now I'm yelling and whispering at the same time across the room if you know what that sounds like! I'm saying "Jamie, Jamieee" I need him to know what's happening, but he already knows. These women are already walking up to him asking about me. He walks up to me and says "Seeeee I told you." As we were standing there a random thought came to me, so I asked Jamie, I said "Hey Jamie, you said this was a paint and sip, but where are the canvases?" He smiled at me and said, "Oh they're on their way, a few of them are stuck in traffic". Eyes like an Owl yet again. I said "They, Them?" He laughed and walked away. That is also a story for another day.

Fast forward 9 months later and I'm making a lot of money in this industry, an industry that I never thought I would be a part of. I'm getting a lot of attention because of my long hair, body, and tattoos. Girls see me working and spending time with other girls and now they want to work with me. I received a pretty big head start because of the people I knew and met along the way. I was in the top 14 percent of grossing adult content creators on OnlyFans. Then I signed my contract and went from a content creator to a full-fledged Pornstar! Signed to an agency that helped me skip the line because women liked not only my appearance but also my innocence. I was "fresh meat" as they call it in the industry…no pun intended.

Life started rough for me. Getting in trouble with the police, failed relationships I put my all into, being an outcast in what felt like real friendships at the time, being the ugly duckling of my family, and the list goes on. Come to think of it, the only reason I even allowed myself into this industry is because I wanted to feel wanted by someone other than the police, and that first night at that paint and sip event, well that was the first time in my life everyone that I was in a room with wanted me. Sounds a little sappy I know, but remember I love love! So much so that Jamie gave me the stage name Luva Boii. I liked it so I kept it.

At this point in my life, I am happy and feeling more free than I've ever felt. I've got friends I never thought I would ever have, and women that used to reject me are now sliding in my DM's. I get noticed everywhere I go, and folks are running after me just to take pictures with me. I feel like a celebrity, I feel like I've got it all. Something is definitely missing though… Love. I never really got over that breakup with Dionna I just distracted myself, I never gave myself a chance to grieve over my grandfather passing away. Not to mention I've completely blocked out of my mind that my grandmother is passing away from brain cancer, on top of the fact that I barely pray anymore. I need to regain some type of structure in my life. (Update: as of today I've lost not only my grandfather but also both of my grandmothers and my aunt, on top of being in jail for a crime I didn't commit and not being able to attend their funerals.

Finally got released and all charges dropped but that wasn't until I lost everything, my Job, my home, my truck, my so-called friends. I'm in the middle of a total life restart.) I'll tell this story very soon!

I needed to gain some structure back into my life. Was this really what I wanted? Not at all! I was living what could be considered most men's dream, and here I am thinking about that white picket fence lifestyle. I want a wife and kids. Never giving my Pops a grandchild to hold before he passed away really got to me. Communication is slowly dying with my mother. No… this won't be how I go out. These industry people don't really love me, they just love the money I make them, or the views they get on their Instagram page when they post themselves with me.

It's time for a change, I can't give up on love. I love it so much! I know my person is out there searching for me just as hard as I'm searching for her. Truth is, as long as I continue to leave God outta my search I'll never find her. So I'm on the search again, having experienced my singleness in a way most folks never do. I'm searching for my person, my woman, my forever, my love, my family! My name is LaTre' and I love love!

I LOVE LOVE!

Understanding the Industry

The Scope of the Adult Entertainment Industry

So you want to be a paid hoe. You wanna be a content creator. You wanna be a pornstar. You are extra horny you think you fuck good and you want to get paid to be a sex symbol. You want to become a part of the adult entertainment industry, or in other words, you wanna do porn. I bet you didn't know that the porn industry is a big ass part of the global economy, with billions of dollars in revenue each year. The internet and digital streaming platforms have turned this industry into something like never before, making adult content more accessible and diverse that anyone can do it. According to recent studies, the porn industry as a whole generates over $100 billion annually, shits crazy right! This figure includes various segments such as videos, camming, live shows, adult toys, cremes, prostitution, sex shops, strip clubs, and sex parties. Who doesn't like a good gang bang am I right? Your favorite publication does!

The industry won't stop growing anytime soon for a few different reasons. Technological advancements have made it easier to produce and distribute content, while changes in societal attitudes have led to greater acceptance of adult entertainment. In other words, it's easy to do and women complained so much about their independence and rights that folks don't judge them the same way they used to. Back in my day, a whore was a whore, now we call them content creators, shits crazy. Regardless, the rise of high-speed internet and big-screen smartphones has also added to the industry's rise, giving horn balls access to content anytime, anywhere, and on any occasion. Plus COVID-19 had people stuck in the house horny as hell, take a guess what they decided to do!

Understanding the world's financial landscape and growth trends is important for anyone considering a career in sex work. The industry's resilience and adaptability to technological changes suggest that it will continue to evolve and grow for many years to come. For prospective performers, staying informed about market trends and consumer fetishes can help them make smart career decisions.

Different Genres and Niches Within Pornography

Pornography caters to a huge array of preferences, fantasies, and fetishes. Mainstream genres include heterosexual, homosexual, lesbian, and bisexual content, so basically straight porn and gay porn. However, there are countless niches, like

BDSM, fetish, amateur, mature, interracial, public, orgy, ebony, and even pregnant each with its own audience and market dynamics. Identifying your niche can help you target the right audience and maximize your appeal. For example, I am a light-skinned man with long curly hair a cut body, and tattoos that stand out, people like to watch me fuck with the sexiest women I can find. The curve in my dick appeals to my female audience and the foreign women I shoot with cater to my male audience.

Each niche has its unique characteristics and appeal. For instance, BDSM (Bondage, Discipline, Sadism, and Masochism) content focuses more so on viewers interested in power dynamics and role-playing scenarios, kinda like 50 Shades of Gray, or rich white men who want to be tied up by an old woman and spanked. Fetish content focuses on specific objects or body parts, such as feet or latex clothing, black pussy, double penetration, or even BBW. Amateur porn, characterized by its raw and unpolished style, appeals to viewers seeking authenticity and relatability, most content creators fall under this category. Amateur has nothing to do with your skill level of fucking or how much fucking experience you have. Mature content features older performers, often highlighting their expertise, experience, and confidence.

Understanding these niches and their audiences is crucial for performers and producers. Market research, including analyzing viewer demographics and preferences, can provide valuable insights. Additionally, engaging with fans through social media and forums can help in identifying trends and building a loyal audience.

Major Players and Production Companies

The industry is dominated by several major production companies known for high-quality content and professional standards. Companies like Vivid Entertainment, Brazzers, Digital Playground, and Bang Bros have established reputations. These companies often set industry standards for production quality, performer treatment, and marketing strategies.

Vivid Entertainment is an OG in the porn game, founded in 1984, they are one of the oldest and most well-known adult film studios. They have produced thousands of high-profile films and have played a crazy big part in shaping the porn industry that we know today. Brazzers, known for its high-definition content and humorous themes, has a massive global audience. Digital Playground is famous for its big-budget productions and cinematic approach to adult films. Bang Bros, with its extensive network of websites, caters to a wide range of niches and preferences.

What do all these companies have in common? Numerous independent producers and studios cater to specific niches. These smaller entities often offer unique and diverse content that appeals to niche audiences. For performers, working with both major companies and independent producers can provide a range of opportunities and experiences.

Familiarizing yourself with these entities can provide insights into the industry's standards and expectations. Networking with professionals from these companies, attending industry events, and staying updated with industry news can help in building valuable connections and advancing your career.

The Legal Landscape

Legal compliance is paramount in the adult entertainment industry. Performers must be at least 18 years old, and production companies are required to verify and document the ages of all participants. This often involves providing government-issued identification and signing affidavits. Ensuring all legal requirements are met protects both performers and producers from legal repercussions.

Age verification processes are strict to prevent exploitation and ensure the legality of the content produced. Companies typically maintain detailed records, including copies of IDs and signed model release forms, to comply with legal requirements. These records must be readily available for inspection by feds.

Performers should be aware of the documentation they need to provide and ensure that their personal information is handled securely. You are in charge of your own well-being. Understanding these legal requirements and adhering to them can be the difference between success and failure in the industry.

Laws Governing Pornography Production and Distribution

Porn has various laws and regulations surrounding it, which differ by country and region. In the United States, federal laws such as 18 U.S.C. § 2257 mandate record-keeping requirements for producers. This law requires producers to maintain detailed records verifying the ages of performers and to make these records available for inspection. So if you are trying to do this, you can't get upset if someone asks for your I.D.

Other countries may have different regulations regarding the production, distribution, and consumption of adult content. For example, the UK has strict regulations on what types of content can be legally produced and distributed. In Japan, censorship laws require the obscuring of genitalia in adult films, which let's be honest, we all hate, but if you ever wanted to know why, well now you know.

Understanding these laws could be crucial to shoot legally and avoiding penalties, like fucking jail. For international performers and producers, staying informed about the regulations in each market they operate in is essential. Legal counsel specializing in the adult entertainment industry can provide guidance and help navigate these complex legal landscapes.

Copyright Issues and Piracy Concerns

Piracy is a significant challenge in the adult entertainment industry. Protecting your content from unauthorized distribution is crucial for maintaining revenue streams. This involves understanding copyright laws and using digital rights management (DRM) tools. Some performers and companies also pursue legal action against piracy to protect their intellectual property. I recommend creating your own production company and putting out all of your films through that new LLC.

Copyright laws protect original works, including adult films, from unauthorized use. Registering your content with copyright authorities can provide legal protection and the ability to pursue legal action against infringers. DRM tools, such as watermarks and encryption, can help prevent unauthorized distribution and track pirated copies.

Performers and producers should be wise in protecting their content. Most folks are stupid and don't understand business. So for the idiots, this includes monitoring online platforms for unauthorized copies, issuing takedown notices, and working with legal professionals to pursue legal action when necessary, making sure you do your paperwork properly so you don't get yourself in a jam.

Gotta idea for a video, copyright that idea, because I'll tell you what will happen. You will put that video out, and get 1 million views, sounds good right? Naw, because if you didn't copyright that video then someone else can create an exact copy of everything you did in that video down to the words and acting, and they'll get 53 million views on the exact same thing. Well if you copyright your content then you could either order a cease & desist, or you could claim their revenue from that content, meaning you make all the money from that video they uploaded using your idea. While piracy cannot be completely eradicated, these measures can help minimize its impact.

Ethical Considerations

Consent and Agency in Adult Film Work

Consent is a cornerstone of ethical adult entertainment. Every performer must give explicit, informed consent for all activities on set. This involves clear communication and agreement on what will be filmed and any boundaries. Ethical practices also include transparency about the nature of the work and respect for performers' autonomy. So if she tells you don't put it in her butt, this means don't put it in her butt.

Performers should feel empowered to communicate their boundaries and preferences openly. Never be afraid to say you don't fuck with something. Production companies should create an environment where consent is prioritized and respected. This includes providing clear information about the scenes being filmed, ensuring that all activities are consensual, and addressing any concerns that arise during production. Keep in mind this is for porn stars, consent is just as important for content creators, it just gets handled a little differently. Still very professional though, at least it should be. I'll go into more detail about this later.

Ensuring informed consent protects performers' rights and contributes to a safer and more respectful industry. Both performers and producers should be committed to upholding these ethical standards.

The Role of Advocacy Groups and Unions

Several organizations advocate for the rights and welfare of adult performers. Groups like the Free Speech Coalition and Performers Availability Screening Services (PASS) provide resources, support, and advocacy. Joining organizations like this can offer protection, networking opportunities, and a platform to voice concerns and drive industry standards.

The Free Speech Coalition (FSC) advocates for the rights of the adult entertainment industry, providing legal support, industry news, and resources. PASS focuses on health and safety, offering a standardized testing system to ensure the sexual health of performers. They are like the union for porn.

These organizations play a crucial role in promoting ethical practices, improving working conditions, and providing support to performers. Engaging with these groups and unions can enhance your career and contribute to positive industry changes.

Addressing Stigma and Societal Perceptions

Porn is often stigmatized, which can affect performers' personal and professional lives. Addressing this stigma involves understanding societal perceptions and developing strategies to manage public image. Engaging in advocacy and education can also help shift societal attitudes towards greater acceptance and respect for adult performers.

Performers may face judgment and discrimination due to

their career choice. Being prepared for these challenges and developing strategies to manage them is essential. This includes maintaining privacy boundaries, managing your public persona, and seeking support from trusted friends and family. Don't let social media get under your skin. Them comments will spank you, and not in a good way.

Educating yourself can also help combat stigma. Engaging in public speaking, writing articles, and participating in discussions about the adult entertainment industry can help challenge misconceptions and promote a more nuanced understanding of the industry and its performers.

Ask Yourself This

Why Do You Want to Become a Pornstar?

Reflecting on your motivations is essential before entering the industry. Whether your reasons are financial, personal, or professional, clarity about your goals can guide your career decisions and help you stay focused and motivated. Why do you wanna do this shit? Most men just wanna brag about getting paid to fuck. Most women need money and use this career to hide being a hoe.

Understanding your motivations can also help you navigate the challenges of the industry. For some, the primary motivation may be financial, seeking a lucrative career that offers flexibility and independence. Others may be driven by a desire for fame, sexual expression, or a passion for performance.

Whatever your reasons, being clear about them can help you set realistic expectations and make informed decisions. It can also guide your career strategy, helping you choose the right opportunities and navigate challenges effectively.

Setting Realistic Expectations and Goals

The porn industry offers various opportunities, but it also comes with challenges. Setting realistic expectations about income, fame, and career longevity can help you navigate the industry more effectively. Establish both short-term and long-term goals to measure your progress and stay motivated.

Understanding the realities of the industry is crucial. While some performers achieve significant fame and financial success, many work steadily without becoming household names. Income can be variable, and the career span of a performer may be limited. Setting realistic expectations can help you navigate these uncertainties and build a sustainable career.

Establishing clear goals can also help you stay focused and motivated. Short-term goals might include gaining experience, building a fan base, or learning new skills. Long-term goals could involve expanding your brand, diversifying your income streams, or transitioning to other roles within the industry.

Evaluating Your Comfort Levels and Boundaries

Self-assessment involves understanding your comfort levels with various aspects of adult entertainment. Evaluate what types of scenes and activities you are comfortable performing and identify your boundaries. This self-awareness is crucial for maintaining your well-being and ensuring a positive experience in the industry.

Consider your comfort levels with different types of scenes, including solo performances, partner scenes, group scenes, and specific fetishes. Be honest with yourself about what you are willing to do and what is off-limits. Communicating these boundaries clearly with producers and directors is essential for maintaining a positive working relationship.

Your boundaries may change over time, and it's important to regularly reassess and communicate them. Staying true to your comfort levels can help you avoid negative experiences and ensure that your career aligns with your values and well-being.

Physical and Mental Preparation

Physical health is crucial in the adult entertainment industry. Regular exercise, a balanced diet, and adequate rest are essential for maintaining your stamina and appearance. Consider working with fitness professionals to develop a regimen that suits your needs and helps you perform at your best.

Maintaining physical health involves more than just appearance. Stamina and flexibility are important for performing demanding scenes. A balanced diet can help you maintain energy levels, while regular exercise can improve your overall health and performance.

Working with fitness professionals, such as personal trainers or nutritionists, can help you develop a personalized fitness and nutrition plan. This can ensure that you are physically prepared for the demands of the industry and can perform at your best.

In my book, *Lifting To Feel Lifted*, I delve deeper into these topics. I provide comprehensive guides on achieving better health, including detailed workout and meal plans. Additionally, I offer insights on how to leverage your transformed body to your advantage, and how to gain that female attention you've been craving.

Mental Health and Emotional Resilience

The industry can be emotionally and mentally demanding. Building emotional resilience and seeking support when needed is essential. Consider therapy or counseling to address any concerns and develop coping strategies for the unique challenges of this career.

Mental health is just as important as physical health. The adult entertainment industry can be stressful and challenging, with potential impacts on self-esteem, relationships, and mental well-being. Building emotional resilience involves developing coping strategies, seeking support, and maintaining a healthy work-life balance.

Therapy or counseling can provide valuable support and tools to manage stress, build resilience, and address any mental health concerns. Having a strong support network, including friends, family, and peers, can also help you navigate the challenges of the industry.

Building a Support Network

Having a support network of friends, family, and industry peers can provide emotional support and practical advice. Building relationships with other performers and industry professionals can also offer insights and opportunities for collaboration.

A strong support network can help you navigate the ups and downs of the industry. Friends and family who understand and support your career choice can provide emotional stability and encouragement. Building relationships with other performers and industry professionals can offer practical advice, mentorship, and opportunities for collaboration.

Engaging with online communities, attending industry events, and joining advocacy groups can also help you connect with peers and build a supportive network. These connections can provide valuable support, advice, and opportunities throughout your career.

Acting and Performance Skills

Acting skills could be considered essential for creating engaging and believable scenes. Consider taking acting classes or workshops to enhance your performance abilities. Understanding basic acting techniques can help you convey emotions and narratives more effectively. It's not exactly necessary but it definitely helps and helps you stand apart.

Acting skills can enhance your performances and make them more engaging for viewers. Taking acting classes or workshops can help you develop techniques for conveying emotions, building characters, and creating compelling scenes. Understanding basic acting principles, such as improvisation, body language, and dialogue delivery, can improve your performance and set you apart from other performers.

Investing in acting training can also open up opportunities in other areas of the entertainment industry, such as mainstream acting or modeling. Building a diverse skill set can enhance your career prospects and provide more opportunities for growth and success.

Sexual Health and Safety Practices

Understanding sexual health and safety practices is crucial. Regular testing for sexually transmitted infections (STIs), using protection, and maintaining open communication with partners is essential for your health and safety. Consider taking courses or workshops on sexual health to stay informed and protected.

Maintaining sexual health involves regular testing, using protection, and staying informed about STI prevention and treatment. Participating in the PASS testing system can ensure that you and your partners are regularly screened for STIs, providing a safer working environment. When I was full-time in the adult industry I was getting tested for everything twice a month, once every 2 weeks. After I got my clean results I refused to have sex with anyone who I was not scheduled to film with, I didn't wanna risk having a negative test before a shoot, and lose any money.

Educating yourself on sexual health and safety is essential, the most important actually. Consider taking courses or workshops on topics such as STI prevention, contraception, and safe sex practices. Staying informed and proactive about your sexual health can protect you and your partners, ensuring a safe and healthy career.

Marketing and Branding Yourself

Building a personal brand is essential in the adult entertainment industry. Develop a unique persona and use social media, websites, and other platforms to promote yourself. Consider working with marketing professionals to create a strategy that highlights your strengths and attracts your target audience.

Marketing and branding are crucial for building a successful career in the adult entertainment industry. Developing a unique persona and consistent brand can help you stand out and attract a loyal fan base. Utilize social media platforms, websites, and other online tools to promote yourself and connect with fans.

Consider working with marketing professionals to develop a comprehensive branding strategy. This can include creating a professional website, managing social media profiles, producing promotional materials, and developing a content strategy. Investing in your brand can enhance your visibility, attract opportunities, and build a sustainable career.

In The Beginning...

Researching and Selecting Production Companies

Researching and selecting reputable production companies is important for a successful and safe career if your planning on being more than a content creator. I'll explain the difference between a pornstar and a content creator in a later chapter. Look for companies with a good track record of treating performers well, producing high-quality content, and adhering to legal and ethical standards. Reading reviews, seeking recommendations from industry peers, and researching company histories can help you identify reputable companies.

Consider things like the company's reputation, production quality, performer treatment, and compliance with legal and ethical standards. Reading reviews and testimonials from other performers can provide valuable insights into the company's practices and working conditions.

Networking with industry professionals and seeking recommendations can also help you identify reputable companies. Attending industry events and engaging with online communities can provide opportunities to connect with experienced performers and producers who can offer advice and recommendations. A good example of a industry event would be the yearly Exxxotica conventions. Lifestyle parties are also a good way to network

Understanding Contracts and Agreements

Contracts and agreements are crucial for protecting your rights and interests. Understand the terms and conditions of any contract before signing. Consider working with a legal professional to review contracts and ensure that they are fair and in your best interest.

Contracts typically outline the terms of your work, including compensation, rights to the content, and obligations of both parties. It's essential to understand these terms and ensure that they are fair and reasonable. Consider working with a legal professional who specializes in the adult entertainment industry to review contracts and provide advice.

Understanding your rights and obligations can help you avoid potential disputes and ensure a positive working relationship with production companies. Being informed and proactive about contracts can protect your interests and contribute to a successful career.

Auditioning and Negotiating Terms

Auditioning for roles involves showcasing your skills and personality. This is where your acting comes into play. It's not all about having sex, some directors are looking for something very specific. Prepare for auditions by understanding the requirements and practicing your performance. The director might want someone who really tries when it comes to their acting ability. If he says act like a schoolgirl who's scared for her strict parents to find out about that bad grade then you need to play the part! It's money in your pocket. Negotiating terms involves discussing compensation, working conditions, and other aspects of the job. Being confident and assertive in negotiations can help you secure favorable terms.

Auditioning is an opportunity to showcase your skills and personality to potential employers. Preparing for auditions involves understanding the requirements, practicing your performance, and presenting yourself professionally. Confidence and preparation can help you make a positive impression and increase your chances of securing roles.

Negotiating terms is an essential skill for securing favorable working conditions and compensation. Be clear about your expectations and be prepared to discuss and negotiate terms such as pay rates, working hours, and scene requirements. Being confident and assertive in negotiations can help you secure better terms and ensure a positive working relationship with production companies.

Producing High-Quality Content

Producing high-quality content is essential for building a successful career. This involves understanding the technical aspects of production, such as lighting, camera work, and editing. Consider investing in equipment and learning production skills to create professional content.

High-quality content requires attention to detail and a commitment to excellence. Understanding the technical aspects of production, such as lighting, camera work, and editing, can enhance the quality of your content and attract a larger audience. Consider investing in professional equipment and learning production skills to create polished and engaging content. You can produce your own high-quality content yourself with good lights a nice background, a high-quality camera, and a working laptop with an internet connection. Phones are a popular device used nowadays for content creation, and the cameras are pretty high quality.

Working with experienced professionals, such as directors, photographers, and editors, can also enhance the quality of your content. Collaborating with professionals who share your vision and standards can help you produce high-quality content that stands out in the competitive adult entertainment industry.

Building a Portfolio and Showreel

A portfolio and showreel are essential tools for showcasing your work and attracting opportunities. Select your best work to create a portfolio that highlights your skills and versatility.

A showreel is a short video compilation of your performances, providing a dynamic way to present your abilities. This is only if you're trying to be more than a content creator.

Building a portfolio involves selecting your best work and presenting it in a professional and organized manner. This can include photos, videos, and other materials that showcase your skills and versatility. A well-crafted portfolio can help you attract opportunities and demonstrate your abilities to potential employers and collaborators.

A showreel is a dynamic way to present your performances. It typically includes short clips from your best scenes, highlighting your skills and versatility. Creating a professional and engaging showreel can enhance your visibility and attract more opportunities.

Marketing and Promoting Your Content

Marketing and promoting your content is crucial for building a fan base and attracting opportunities. Utilize social media, websites, and other platforms to promote your work. Engaging with fans and building a loyal following can enhance your visibility and success.

Effective marketing involves utilizing various platforms to promote your content and connect with fans. Social media platforms, such as Instagram, Twitter, and OnlyFans, provide opportunities to share content, engage with fans, and build a loyal following. Creating a professional website can also enhance your online presence and provide a platform for promoting your work.

Engaging with fans is crucial for building a loyal following. Responding to comments, hosting live streams, and offering exclusive content can enhance your connection with fans and build a strong fan base. Developing a comprehensive marketing strategy can enhance your visibility, attract opportunities, and contribute to a successful career.

Safety, Understanding, and Preventing Exploitation

Understanding and preventing exploitation is crucial for maintaining your safety and well-being. Be aware of your rights and seek support from industry organizations if you encounter exploitation or abuse. Developing a strong support network and staying informed about industry standards can help you navigate the industry safely.

Exploitation and abuse are serious concerns in the adult entertainment industry. Being aware of your rights and seeking support from industry organizations can help you navigate these challenges. Organizations such as the Free Speech Coalition and PASS provide resources and support for performers, helping them navigate the industry safely.

Developing a strong support network can also provide valuable protection and support. Connecting with other performers, seeking advice from experienced professionals, and staying informed about industry standards can help you navigate the industry safely and effectively.

Ensuring Financial Security and Stability

Ensuring financial security and stability is crucial for a successful career. Develop a financial plan that includes budgeting, saving, and investing. Consider working with a financial advisor to manage your income and plan for the future. Many younger performers get excited about the money they are making and spend it all up, but keep in mind that body won't look the same forever. In 20 years you gonna need something to fall back on. I suggest taking the production company we created in the earlier chapter of this book and using it to sign other performers.

Financial security and stability are essential for a successful and sustainable career. Developing a financial plan involves budgeting, saving, and investing to ensure that you can manage your income and plan for the future. Consider working with a financial advisor who specializes in the adult entertainment industry to develop a comprehensive financial plan.

Building multiple income streams, such as content sales, live shows, and merchandise, can enhance your financial stability and security. Diversifying your income sources can provide a stable and reliable income, helping you navigate the financial uncertainties of the industry.

Maintaining Professional and Personal Boundaries

Maintaining professional and personal boundaries is crucial for your well-being and success. Establish clear boundaries between your work and personal life, and communicate them clearly to others. Developing strategies to manage your public image and privacy can help you navigate the industry safely and effectively.

Maintaining professional and personal boundaries involves establishing clear boundaries between your work and personal life. This can include setting limits on the types of scenes you perform, managing your public image, and maintaining privacy boundaries. Communicating these boundaries clearly to others can help you navigate the industry safely and effectively.

Developing strategies to manage your public image and privacy is also essential. This can include using a stage name, managing your social media presence, and setting limits on the information you share publicly. Maintaining a healthy work-life balance and protecting your privacy can enhance your well-being and contribute to a successful career.

Making This Shit Last

Diversifying Your Income Streams

Diversifying your income streams is essential for building a sustainable career. Consider checking out different revenue sources, such as content sales, live shows, merchandise, and endorsements. Developing multiple income streams can enhance your financial stability and security. Onlyfans is just one source.

Exploring different revenue sources can enhance your financial stability and provide more growth opportunities. This can include selling content through platforms like OnlyFans or Clips4Sale, performing live shows or camming, selling merchandise, and securing endorsements or sponsorships.

Building multiple income streams can provide a stable and reliable income, helping you navigate the financial uncertainties of the industry. Diversifying your income sources can also enhance your career prospects and provide more opportunities for growth and success.

Investing in Your Brand

Investing in your brand is important for building a successful career. Develop a unique persona and use marketing strategies to promote your brand. Consider working with marketing professionals to create a comprehensive branding strategy that highlights your strengths and attracts your target audience.

Investing in your brand also includes putting the money you make from the industry back into the industry. So if you made $500 filming on a $50 camera, then go buy a $500 camera and make $5000. Get your lights, and get a green screen. You can get rope, masks, and bondage. Basically, get anything that will help add diversity to your videos and feed a certain niche. As a woman, you might purchase toys or lingerie. Massage tables are good tools. You can advertise body rubs and give discounts for content creators, now your getting booked and paid.

Investing in your brand involves developing a unique persona and utilizing marketing strategies to promote yourself. This can include creating a professional website, managing social media profiles, producing promotional materials, and developing a content strategy.

Consider working with marketing professionals to develop

a comprehensive branding strategy. Investing in your brand can enhance your visibility, attract opportunities, and build a sustainable career. A strong personal brand can set you apart from other performers and provide more opportunities for growth and success.

Planning for the Future and Career Longevity

We touched on this subject a little bit already, but planning for the future and career longevity is essential for a successful career. Develop a long-term career plan that includes goals, strategies, and contingencies. Consider exploring opportunities for growth and development, such as transitioning to other roles within the industry or expanding your brand.

Developing a long-term career plan involves setting goals, developing strategies, and planning for contingencies. This can include exploring opportunities for growth and development, such as transitioning to other roles within the industry, expanding your brand, or pursuing other interests.

Planning for the future and career longevity can enhance your success and stability in the industry. You gotta be proactive and strategic about your career, that will help you navigate challenges, seize opportunities, and build a sustainable and successful career. It's easy to become a legend in this industry, just look good, be different, and do good business.

The adult entertainment industry comes with unique stressors. Developing coping strategies and seeking support when needed is essential for your well-being. Consider therapy or counseling to address any concerns and develop coping strategies for the unique challenges of this career. This shit can get hard, this shit can get lonely, you gotta be a strong person to deal with this type of stress, it's not normal stress.

Coping with industry-specific stressors involves developing strategies to manage stress and seeking support when needed. This can include practicing self-care, maintaining a healthy work-life balance, and seeking support from friends, family, and professionals. This might prove to be difficult for some, mainly because this isn't typically the industry families tend to support, but I assure you, you have options!

Consider therapy or counseling to address any concerns and develop coping strategies for the unique challenges of this career. Building emotional resilience and seeking support can enhance your well-being and help you navigate the challenges of the industry.

Dealing with Public Scrutiny and Stigma

Public scrutiny and stigma are challenges that many adult performers face. I personally don't give a fuck what people think of me, but developing strategies to manage public perception and protect your privacy can be considered essential. This might be hard considering you're fucking on the internet for money, but engaging in advocacy and education can help shift societal attitudes toward greater acceptance and respect for adult performers.

Dealing with public scrutiny and stigma involves developing strategies to manage public perception and protect your privacy. This can include maintaining privacy boundaries, managing your public persona, and seeking support from trusted friends and family.

Engaging in advocacy and education efforts can also help combat stigma. Participating in public speaking, writing articles, and engaging in discussions about the adult entertainment industry can help challenge misconceptions and promote a more nuanced understanding of the industry and its performers.

That a more politically correct approach, an even better way to think of it is simple... Fuck People! An old friend once told me that if that person isn't fucking, feeding, or financing you then they can take how they feel and shove it up their ass.

Building a Supportive Community

Building a supportive community of friends, family, and industry peers can provide emotional support and practical advice. Developing relationships with other performers and industry professionals can offer insights and opportunities for collaboration.

A supportive community can provide valuable support and advice throughout your career. Connecting with other performers, seeking advice from experienced professionals, and building relationships with industry peers can enhance your support network. Surround yourself with like-minded individuals, this will help with your support system.

Engaging with online communities, attending industry events, and joining advocacy groups can also help you build a supportive community. These connections can provide valuable support, advice, and opportunities throughout your career.

Staying Updated with Industry Trends and Technologies

The adult entertainment industry is constantly evolving. Staying updated with industry trends and technologies is essential for maintaining your competitiveness. Consider attending industry events, reading industry publications, and engaging with online communities to stay informed.

Staying updated with industry trends and technologies can enhance your competitiveness and provide more growth opportunities. This can include attending industry events, reading industry publications, and engaging with online communities.

Understanding the latest trends and technologies can help you stay informed and adapt to changes in the industry. Staying updated can also provide opportunities for growth and development, enhancing your success and stability in the industry.

Expanding Your Skill Set and Versatility

Expanding your skill set and versatility is crucial for building a successful career. Consider taking classes or workshops to develop new skills and enhance your performance abilities. Building a diverse skill set can provide more opportunities for growth and success. This might sound weird, but you wanna know what sounds even weirder? A woman that cant ride dick! You can be taught how to do this.

Expanding your skill set involves developing new skills and enhancing your performance abilities. This can include taking classes or workshops on acting, production, marketing, and other relevant areas.

Building a diverse skill set can enhance your career prospects and provide more opportunities for growth and success. Being versatile and adaptable can help you navigate challenges, seize opportunities, and build a sustainable and successful career.

Seeking Mentorship and Professional Guidance

Seeking mentorship and professional guidance can provide valuable support and advice throughout your career. This book is an example of seeking guidance. Connecting with experienced professionals and mentors can offer insights and opportunities for growth and development.

Mentorship and professional guidance can provide valuable support and advice throughout your career. Connecting with experienced professionals and mentors can offer insights and opportunities for growth and development.

Engaging with industry organizations, attending events, and seeking recommendations can help you connect with potential mentors and professionals. Building these relationships can enhance your support network and contribute to your success and stability in the industry.

Be Smart

Establishing a Professional Routine

Creating a consistent work schedule can help you manage your time effectively and maintain a healthy work-life balance. Determine the number of hours you plan to dedicate to work each week, including filming, content creation, marketing, and administrative tasks. Having a set schedule can help you stay organized and productive.

A well-structured work schedule allows you to allocate time for various tasks, ensuring that you can meet deadlines and achieve your goals. This includes setting aside time for filming, editing, marketing, and engaging with fans. Balancing work and personal time is crucial for maintaining your well-being and preventing burnout.

Consider using productivity tools and apps to help you manage your schedule. Calendar apps, task management tools, and time-tracking software can help you stay on top of your tasks and ensure that you are using your time efficiently.

Setting Professional Boundaries

Setting professional boundaries is essential for maintaining your well-being and ensuring that your work does not interfere with your personal life. Establish clear boundaries between your work and personal time, and communicate these boundaries to your colleagues, fans, and family members.

Professional boundaries can include setting limits on the hours you are available for work-related activities, such as filming, marketing, and responding to fan messages. It can also involve setting boundaries around the types of content you are willing to create and the level of interaction you have with fans.

Clear communication of your boundaries is essential for maintaining a healthy work-life balance. Make sure to communicate your boundaries to your colleagues, fans, and family members to ensure that they respect your time and personal space.

Budgeting and Financial Planning

Touching on this category will be a habit throughout this book, it's important. Effective budgeting and financial planning are crucial for ensuring your financial stability and security. Develop a budget that includes your income and expenses, and track your spending to ensure that you are living within your means. Consider setting aside a portion of your income for savings and investments to secure your financial future, and always reinvest in your brand.

A well-structured budget can help you manage your income and expenses, ensuring that you can cover your living expenses, save for the future, and invest in your career. Regularly review and adjust your budget to account for changes in your income and expenses.

Consider working with a financial advisor who specializes in the adult entertainment industry. A financial advisor can help you develop a comprehensive financial plan that includes budgeting, saving, investing, and planning for retirement.

Understanding Taxes and Legal Obligations

Understanding your tax and legal obligations is essential for ensuring that you comply with the law and protect your rights. Familiarize yourself with the tax requirements for independent contractors and self-employed individuals, and ensure that you are properly reporting your income and expenses.

Tax obligations can vary depending on your location and the nature of your work. It is important to keep accurate records of your income and expenses and to file your taxes on time. Consider working with a tax professional who understands the specific tax requirements for adult performers to ensure that you comply with the law.

In addition to taxes, it is important to understand your legal obligations and rights as an adult performer. This includes understanding the terms of your contracts, your rights to your content, and the legal protections available to you. Consider working with a legal professional who specializes in the adult entertainment industry to ensure that you are informed and protected.

Protecting Your Intellectual Property

Protecting your intellectual property is essential for ensuring that you retain control over your content and receive the compensation you deserve. Understand your rights to your content and take steps to protect your intellectual property from unauthorized use and distribution.

Intellectual property protection involves registering your content with copyright authorities, using watermarks and other protective measures, and taking legal action against unauthorized use of your content. Consider working with a legal professional who specializes in intellectual property law to ensure that your rights are protected.

In addition to legal protections, consider using technology to protect your content. Digital rights management (DRM) tools, watermarks, and secure distribution platforms can help you protect your content from piracy and unauthorized distribution.

Networking with Industry Professionals

Networking with industry professionals is essential for building a successful and sustainable career. Attend industry events, join professional organizations, and engage with online communities to connect with other performers, producers, and industry professionals.

Networking can provide valuable opportunities for collaboration, mentorship, and career growth. Building relationships with industry professionals can help you gain insights into the industry, access new opportunities, and develop your skills and knowledge. Be careful though, make sure you have a good filter for bullshit, there are a lot of fake people in this industry and they will gladly use you to further their own careers.

Consider joining professional organizations, such as the Free Speech Coalition or the Adult Performer Advocacy Committee, to connect with other performers and industry professionals. Engaging with online communities, such as forums and social media groups, can also provide valuable networking opportunities.

Collaborating with Other Performers

Collaborating with other performers can enhance your visibility, expand your audience, and provide new growth opportunities. Seek out opportunities to work with other performers, such as co-starring in scenes, participating in joint projects, or creating collaborative content. It's kinda like when a musician does a feature with a bigger artist, he now has access to that artist's fan base, which gives that musician a chance to make an impression and grow. How many of us wouldn't want a feature from Drake?

Collaborating will help you the most outta everything, that's how I was able to get so popular so fast. Women see you working with other women and it makes them want to work with you. It is a money-grabbing industry filled with people not afraid to have sex with strangers.

Collaboration can provide valuable exposure and help you reach new audiences. Working with other performers can also provide opportunities to learn new skills, share knowledge, and build a supportive community.

When collaborating with other performers, ensure that you communicate clearly and establish mutual expectations. Developing positive and professional relationships with your collaborators can enhance your reputation and contribute to a successful career.

Building Positive Relationships with Fans

Building positive relationships with your fans is essential for maintaining a loyal and engaged audience. Engage with your fans through social media, live streams, and other platforms to build a strong connection and enhance your visibility.

Engaging with your fans involves responding to comments, hosting live streams, and offering exclusive content. Building a loyal and engaged fan base can enhance your visibility, attract opportunities, and contribute to your financial success.

Consider using fan engagement tools, such as fan clubs, membership platforms, and interactive content, to enhance your connection with your fans. Providing exclusive content, behind-the-scenes access, and personalized interactions can help you build a strong and loyal fan base.

Transitioning to Other Roles within the Industry

Transitioning to other roles within the adult entertainment industry can provide new opportunities for growth and development. Consider exploring roles such as directing, producing, writing, or marketing to diversify your skills and expand your career.

Transitioning to other roles can provide valuable opportunities for growth and development. Exploring roles such as directing, producing, writing, or marketing can help you diversify your skills and enhance your career prospects.

Consider taking classes or workshops to develop the skills needed for your desired role. Building a diverse skill set can enhance your career prospects and provide more opportunities for growth and success.

Pursuing Opportunities Outside the Industry

Pursuing opportunities outside the adult entertainment industry can give you some growth opportunities. You should think about exploring interests and passions that align with your skills and values, and seek out opportunities to transition to new careers.

Transitioning to a new career outside the adult entertainment industry can provide valuable opportunities for growth and development. Exploring interests and passions that align with your skills and values can help you identify new career paths and opportunities.

Consider taking classes or pursuing additional education to develop the skills needed for your desired career. Building a diverse skill set and seeking mentorship and guidance can enhance your career prospects and help you successfully transition to a new career.

Planning for Retirement and Long-Term Goals

Planning for retirement and long-term goals is essential for ensuring your financial security and stability. Develop a long-term financial plan that includes saving for retirement, investing, and planning for future expenses.

A well-structured financial plan can help you ensure that you have the resources needed to retire comfortably and achieve your long-term goals. Consider working with a financial advisor who specializes in the adult entertainment industry to develop a comprehensive retirement plan.

In addition to financial planning, consider setting long-term goals for your career and personal life. Developing a clear vision for your future can help you stay focused and motivated, and provide a roadmap for achieving your goals.

If Your Gonna Do It, Then Do It

Supporting Performer Rights and Welfare

Engaging in advocacy and activism is essential for promoting performer rights and welfare. Consider participating in advocacy efforts, such as public speaking, writing articles, and engaging in discussions about the adult entertainment industry.

Advocacy and activism can help challenge misconceptions, promote a more nuanced understanding of the industry, and support efforts to improve performer rights and welfare. Engaging in advocacy efforts can also provide valuable opportunities for networking and career growth.

Consider joining advocacy organizations, such as the Free Speech Coalition or the Adult Performer Advocacy Committee, to support efforts to improve performer rights and welfare. Participating in advocacy efforts can help you make a positive impact on the industry and support your fellow performers. I didn't, I worked with who I worked with but for the most part, I minded my business and stayed to myself. This helped me and hurt me at the same time.

Promoting Health and Safety Standards

Promoting health and safety standards is essential for ensuring a safe and healthy working environment for performers. Support efforts to improve health and safety standards in the industry, such as advocating for regular STI testing, promoting safe sex practices, and supporting mental health resources.

Health and safety standards are crucial for ensuring that performers can work in a safe and healthy environment. Advocating for regular STI and STD testing, promoting safe sex practices, and supporting mental health resources can help improve the overall well-being of performers. Don't be trifling! You'll make a lot more money if you're known as a clean person.

Consider participating in initiatives and campaigns that promote health and safety standards in the industry. Engaging with organizations that support health and safety efforts can help you make a positive impact on the industry and support your fellow performers. A good example of this is that nigga GucciThirdLeg, he got burnt and started burning others! Now there are people that will never work with him again. Also there are people that refuse to watch his videos or the videos of anyone he worked with.

Providing guidance and support to new performers can help them navigate the industry and build successful careers. Consider offering mentorship and sharing your knowledge and experience with new performers to help them succeed.

Mentorship and guidance can provide valuable support to new performers, helping them navigate the industry's challenges and build successful careers. Sharing your knowledge and experience can help new performers avoid common pitfalls and achieve their goals.

Consider participating in mentorship programs or offering one-on-one support to new performers. Building a supportive community can enhance the overall well-being of performers and contribute to a more positive and successful industry.

Sharing your knowledge and experience with new performers can help them develop their skills and build successful careers. Consider offering workshops, writing articles, or creating educational content to share your insights and expertise.

Educational content can provide valuable resources for new performers, helping them develop their skills and navigate the industry. Sharing your knowledge and experience can help new performers build successful careers and contribute to a more knowledgeable and skilled industry.

Consider creating educational content, such as articles, videos, or workshops, to share your insights and expertise with new performers. Providing valuable resources and support can help new performers succeed and enhance the overall well-being of the industry. This book is a great example of making educational content. This book will help a lot of people, and also touches on topics in the industry other books don't.

Advocating for Ethical Practices And Promoting Positive Industry Change

I don't care who you are or what part you play in this industry, everyone should be doing this. Advocating for ethical practices in the adult entertainment industry is essential for promoting a positive and respectful working environment. Being uncomfortable during a shoot is the worst, male or female it doesn't matter. Support efforts to improve industry standards, such as advocating for fair pay, respectful treatment, and ethical production practices.

Ethical practices are crucial for ensuring a positive and respectful working environment for performers. Advocating for fair pay, respectful treatment, and ethical production practices can help improve the overall well-being of performers and enhance the industry's reputation.

Consider participating in initiatives and campaigns that promote ethical practices in the industry. Engaging with organizations that support ethical practices can help you make a positive impact on the industry and support your fellow performers.

Supporting industry organizations and initiatives is essential for promoting positive change and improving performer rights and welfare. Think about joining and supporting organizations that advocate for performer rights, health and safety standards, and ethical practices.

Who The Fuck Are You?

Creating a Personal Brand

Your Unique Selling Proposition, or USP, is what sets you apart from other performers in the adult entertainment industry. It could be a specific talent, a unique look, a particular style of content, or a distinctive personality trait. Defining your USP is crucial for creating a personal brand that stands out and resonates with your audience.

Take the time to reflect on what makes you unique. Consider what your fans love most about you and what you enjoy most about your work. This self-awareness will help you articulate your USP and incorporate it into your branding strategy.

Developing a Consistent Brand Identity

Consistency is key when it comes to branding. Develop a cohesive brand identity that reflects your USP and resonates with your target audience. This includes your stage name, logo, color scheme, and overall aesthetic. Your brand identity should be reflected across all your platforms, from social media profiles to your website and promotional materials.

Your brand identity should also be evident in your content. Whether you're producing videos, photos, or written content, make sure it aligns with your brand's look and feel. Consistency helps build trust and recognition among your audience, making it easier for them to connect with you.

Leveraging Social Media

Social media is a powerful tool for expanding your reach and building a loyal fan base. Choose platforms that align with your brand and where your target audience is most active. Regularly post engaging content, interact with your fans, and use hashtags and collaborations to increase your visibility.

Each social media platform has its own strengths and user base, so tailor your content to each platform. For example, Instagram is great for visual content, Twitter (X) is excellent for real-time updates and conversations, and TikTok is ideal for short, engaging videos. Understanding the nuances of each platform will help you maximize your reach.

Speaking Of X

When it comes to promoting your OnlyFans or Pornhub content, don't underestimate the power of X, formerly known as Twitter. This platform is a goldmine for driving traffic and increasing the amount of money you can make. It's all about strategy and understanding what your audience wants. A simple 30-second teaser clip, paired with a link to a longer three-minute video, can work wonders.

Here's how it works: Post a 30-second snippet of your latest scene on X. Keep it spicy enough to grab attention but don't show everything, unless you truly just don't give a fuck. Me personally you gotta pay to see me naked, no Twitter freebies. Add a catchy caption and a call to action, like "Want to see more, click the link for the full video!" I even had success by saying something like this: "Me and (whoever else is in the scene) Linked up! Wanna see what happens? Click the link" The link will take them to the full 3-minute clip, or I might have a 20-minute video for them depending on what I have ready to release and the workload I've given myself. Include the link to your OnlyFans or Pornhub page. That little taste of your content is enough to pique curiosity and drive viewers to your full-length videos, where they can subscribe or make purchases.

The key is consistency and engagement. Interact with your followers, reply to comments, and retweet relevant content. Make sure your profile is well-branded and links directly to your subscription platforms. By keeping an active presence on X, you keep your audience engaged and constantly remind them of the premium content waiting for them. It's a simple yet effective strategy that turns casual viewers into paying fans.

Collaborating with Influencers

Collaborating with influencers can help you reach new audiences and enhance your credibility. Look for influencers whose brand aligns with yours and who have a significant following among your target audience. Collaborations can take many forms, from co-starring in content to shout-outs and joint giveaways. This is not the same as collaborating with other performers. This is non-adult content that will push traffic to your adult content. It's time to learn how to be more than a paid hoe.

When collaborating with influencers, ensure that the partnership is mutually beneficial and that both parties are clear on the expectations and deliverables. Effective collaborations can significantly boost your visibility and fan base. Be careful though, a lot of these people are damaged and will jump into a relationship with you just because you're what's popping right now. My suggestion is don't get into a relationship while you are in this industry unless it is with the person you're filming with, and you all only film with each other.

Building a Loyal Fan Base

A loyal fan base is one of your most valuable assets. Engage with your fans regularly through social media, fan clubs, and live events. Show appreciation for their support by responding to comments, hosting Q&A sessions, and offering exclusive content. Go live on Instagram or whatever platforms you use the most. Just interact with them, they'll love you for it and it will do nothing but help you in the long run.

Building a community around your brand fosters a sense of belonging among your fans, making them more likely to support you long-term. A great example of this is someone who isn't even a pornstar but has a cult following. His name is Kai Cenat, his fans will ride for him no matter what. Why? Easy, because he cares and caters to his audience. He didn't create his brand by himself, he created his brand with his fans. Now they love each other for life! Consider creating a membership platform where fans can subscribe for exclusive content and perks. Twitch is a platform that has already been put in place for us if you're not interested in creating your own website from scratch. This not only generates additional income but also strengthens your relationship with your most dedicated fans.

Giving Back to the Community

Giving back to the community can enhance your brand's reputation and build goodwill among your fans. Consider participating in charity events, supporting causes that are important to you, or creating content that raises awareness about social issues. Fan giveaways are also very popular.

Engaging in philanthropic activities shows that you care about more than just your career, which can resonate with your fans and inspire loyalty. Additionally, it can open up opportunities for positive publicity and collaborations with other like-minded individuals and organizations.

Setting Long-Term Goals

Setting long-term goals is essential for maintaining direction and motivation in your career. These goals can include financial targets, career milestones, personal development objectives, and retirement plans. In fact, I encourage everyone to have a retirement plan, because doing this forever is just not an option. Having clear, achievable goals helps you stay focused and measure your progress.

Regularly review and adjust your goals as needed, though I'm sure that goes without saying. The adult entertainment industry gets crazy, and staying adaptable is important for long-term success. Be open to exploring new opportunities and pivoting when necessary to align with your evolving interests and market trends, but don't give up your soul, morals, or values for a lil piece of change. I've seen straight men take a dick in the butt because they saw how much money it paid. Don't through away your boundaries because you need a couple of dollars in your pockets... dat shit gay. Don't be gay for pay!

Preparing for Life After the Industry

It's important to consider what life will look like after your career in the adult entertainment industry. Start planning early for your transition by developing skills and exploring interests that could lead to new career opportunities. This might include pursuing education, gaining certifications, or building a business. Don't get out into the world and the only skill you got is fucking, you'll be shit outta luck.

Consider working with a career coach or mentor to help you navigate this transition. They can provide valuable insights and support as you explore new paths and prepare for the next chapter of your life. Having a clear plan for the future can provide peace of mind and ensure that you're prepared for whatever comes next.

As you build your career, strive to become a positive role model within the industry. This involves conducting yourself with professionalism, treating others with respect, and using your platform to advocate for positive change. Your actions can inspire others and contribute to a more respectful and supportive industry environment.

When I say role model I'm not talking about for kids. I mean someone who is known for professionalism and does good business. When they mention your name they say things like, "he's so respectful" or "I never have to worry about anything when I work with him".

Being a role model also means being honest and transparent about the realities of the industry. Sharing your experiences and challenges can help aspiring performers make informed decisions and navigate their own careers more effectively.

Consider how you can make a lasting difference in the industry. This might involve mentoring new performers, advocating for policy changes, or supporting organizations that promote performer rights and welfare. Your contributions can have a meaningful impact on the industry and help create a better environment for future performers.

Engaging in activities that support positive change not only benefits the industry but also enhances your legacy. Being remembered for your contributions and advocacy efforts can be a source of pride and fulfillment as you reflect on your career.

Get Dat Bread Get Dat Head With Onlyfans

Understanding OnlyFans

OnlyFans is a content subscription platform that allows creators to earn money by sharing exclusive content with their subscribers. It has gained popularity in the adult entertainment industry as a way for performers to monetize their content directly from fans.

Creators can create a profile on OnlyFans and set a subscription price for access to their content. Subscribers pay a monthly fee to view exclusive photos, videos, and other content posted by creators. OnlyFans takes a percentage of the earnings, and creators receive the rest.

Create a compelling profile that highlights your brand and personality. Use a catchy username and profile picture to attract potential subscribers. Customize your bio and introduction to give fans a preview of what they can expect.

Decide what type of content you want to offer on OnlyFans. This could include photos, videos, live streams, behind-the-scenes footage, and exclusive chats with fans. Tailor your content strategy to your audience's preferences and interests.

Utilize social media platforms, personal websites, and other channels to promote your OnlyFans profile. Share teaser content, exclusive offers, and behind-the-scenes glimpses to entice potential subscribers. Engage with your audience and encourage them to subscribe for exclusive content.

Collaborate with other creators on OnlyFans or related platforms to cross-promote each other's profiles. Collaborations can introduce you to new audiences and expand your subscriber base. Choose collaborators whose content aligns with yours to attract relevant subscribers.

Determine your subscription price based on the value of your content and what your audience is willing to pay. Consider offering tiered subscription options with varying levels of access and perks to appeal to different segments of your audience.

In addition to subscriptions, offer additional services and perks to monetize your content further. This could include custom content requests, personalized shout-outs, private chats, merchandise sales, and exclusive live events. Diversifying your revenue streams can increase your earnings potential.

Engage with your fans regularly by responding to messages, comments, and feedback. Make them feel valued and appreciated by offering personalized interactions and exclusive content. Building strong relationships with your fans can lead to long-term subscriptions and loyal support.

Foster a sense of community among your subscribers by hosting live events, interactive Q&A sessions, and fan polls. Encourage fans to interact with each other and create a supportive and engaging environment. A strong community can enhance fan loyalty and retention.

Maintain a consistent posting schedule and deliver high-quality content to keep subscribers engaged and satisfied. Regularly update your profile with fresh content, promotions, and announcements to maintain interest and attract new subscribers.

Use analytics tools provided by OnlyFans to track your performance, subscriber growth, and revenue. Analyze metrics such as engagement rates, subscription renewals, and content preferences to optimize your strategy and maximize earnings.

Familiarize yourself with OnlyFans' terms of service, content guidelines, and legal requirements. Ensure that your content complies with copyright laws, age verification standards, and other regulatory obligations. Protect your intellectual property and privacy rights while operating on the platform.

Prioritize the safety and security of your content and personal information on OnlyFans. Use secure passwords, enable two-factor authentication, and be cautious of phishing attempts and scams. Report any suspicious activity or violations to OnlyFans support for assistance.

Implement strategies to maximize your earnings potential on OnlyFans. This includes optimizing your pricing strategy, promoting exclusive content and offers, leveraging collaborations and partnerships, and continuously engaging with your audience to drive subscriptions and renewals.

Invest in your growth and success on OnlyFans by reinvesting earnings into marketing, content production, and audience engagement initiatives. Explore new content formats, marketing channels, and monetization strategies to expand your reach and increase revenue streams.

Get Paid From Pornhub

Pornhub is one of the largest and most popular adult content websites globally, attracting millions of visitors daily. It offers a platform for performers, studios, and content creators to share and monetize adult videos and other content.

How To Get The Money

Creators can upload their videos to Pornhub and earn money through various monetization methods, including ad revenue, premium subscriptions, tips, and merchandise sales. Understanding how the platform operates is essential for maximizing earning potential.

Sign up for a performer account on Pornhub to start uploading and monetizing your content. Complete your profile with a compelling bio, profile picture, and relevant tags to attract viewers.

Upload high-quality videos to Pornhub that appeal to your target audience. Use engaging titles, descriptions, and tags to optimize search visibility and attract viewers. Consider creating a content schedule to maintain consistency and attract repeat viewers.

Earn money through ad revenue generated from ads displayed on your videos. Optimize your videos for ad placements and engage viewers to increase ad impressions and earnings. Offer premium subscriptions on Pornhub to provide exclusive access to your content, ad-free viewing, and other perks. Set subscription prices and promote your premium content to attract subscribers. Encourage viewers to tip or donate to support your work. Provide incentives such as exclusive content, personalized shout-outs, or virtual gifts for generous tippers.

Promote your Pornhub profile and videos on social media platforms to attract more viewers. Share teaser clips, behind-the-scenes footage, and promotional offers to entice followers to visit your Pornhub page. Collaborate with other creators or studios on Pornhub for cross-promotion. Share each other's content, participate in joint promotions, and engage in mutual support to reach a wider audience and boost viewership.

Engage with your audience on Pornhub by responding to comments, messages, and feedback. Encourage discussions, ask for feedback, and create a welcoming and interactive community.

Live Shows and Events

Host live shows, Q&A sessions, and virtual events on Pornhub to engage with fans in real time. Offer special incentives and exclusive content during live events to encourage participation and boost viewer engagement. If you throw your own parties then you're the boss. You pay the people that help, they don't pay you. Once you get popular enough, you won't even have to fuck for money.

You can throw live sex shows, book strippers and prostitutes around the area, give them a flat fee or allow them to work for tips, and invite as many people as you can, hire a private promoter. Most people are interested in this lifestyle but because it's so extreme they tend to turn away. Make it seem easy for them. Make these men think that if they come to your party they gonna get some pussy from one of the girls for free. Shit, they just might! Swingers parties and lifestyle parties are very popular. I'm currently a part of a team that throws parties like these, we actually own the largest Glory Hole location on the eastern shore. Men love it! Come up with some great ideas for your events and you'll make a lot of money. If you have your own space, hosting lifestyle parties is another way to grow your audience, you can have peep shows and places for swingers to have sex freely.

Use Pornhub's analytics tools to track performance metrics such as views, engagement, earnings, and subscriber growth.

Analyze data to identify trends, optimize content strategy, and make data-driven decisions. Optimize your content based on performance data and viewer feedback. Experiment with different content formats, topics, and styles to identify what resonates most with your audience and drives higher engagement and earnings.

Adhere to Pornhub's content guidelines, terms of service, and legal requirements. Ensure that your content complies with copyright laws, age verification standards, and community guidelines to avoid penalties or account suspension.

Protect your safety and privacy on Pornhub by safeguarding personal information, using secure passwords, and being cautious of scams or phishing attempts. Report any suspicious activity or violations to Pornhub support for assistance.

Implement strategies to maximize earnings on Pornhub, such as optimizing ad placements, promoting premium content, encouraging tips and donations, and leveraging promotional opportunities.

Focus on growing your audience on Pornhub by creating compelling content, engaging with viewers, promoting your profile, and leveraging cross-promotion and collaboration opportunities. Continuously monitor performance metrics and adjust strategies to drive growth and maximize earning potential.

Enhancements and Sexual Health

Male

When it comes to boosting male performance, you've got a range of options—natural and not-so-natural, but sometimes you gotta get creative. Here's the comprehensive guide, covering everything from herbs and supplements to synthetic aids that might catch your eye.

Natural Supplements

Maca Root: This root from the Andes has been touted for its libido-boosting properties and overall vitality enhancement. Often referred to as a natural aphrodisiac, maca root is said to help improve stamina and energy levels. It's been used traditionally to enhance sexual function and fertility. While research is still catching up, many find maca root beneficial for overall well-being.

Horny Goat Weed: Despite its funny name, horny goat weed is known for helping with sexual desire and erectile problems. It has a special ingredient called icariin, which helps improve blood flow and boost libido. Icariin works by stopping an enzyme that limits blood flow, which helps you feel more aroused and improves sexual performance. It might also help with bone health by making bones stronger. However, you should be careful with how much you take, because too much can cause side effects like dizziness, nausea, and upset stomach.

Libido-Max: This supplement combines various herbs and nutrients that are said to support sexual health and performance. It aims to boost libido, improve erectile function, and increase energy levels. Users report varied results, so it's essential to evaluate how it works for you personally.

Fenugreek: Known for its role in traditional medicine, fenugreek may help enhance testosterone levels and support sexual health. It's often used to improve libido and stamina. Fenugreek's benefits for male performance are supported by some studies, though more research is needed.

Honey Packs: While not as widely discussed, honey packs have been used in various cultures for their supposed aphrodisiac properties. Honey itself is packed with nutrients and has been linked to improved sexual function in some traditional practices.

Iguana and Iguana Soup: In some cultures, especially in the Aruba, iguana is believed to be an elixir for male performance. The meat is rich in proteins and nutrients, which are said to boost energy and stamina. Iguana soup is thought to enhance sexual vitality and improve performance. While these claims are rooted in tradition, it's worth noting that scientific evidence is limited.

Mamajuana: This traditional Dominican drink, made from rum, red wine, honey, and a mix of herbs and spices, is known for its purported aphrodisiac qualities. Mamajuana is believed to enhance sexual performance and overall vitality. It's important to note that mamajuana is not to be confused with marijuana. Like iguana soup, its effects are mostly anecdotal, but it has a rich cultural history of being used as a sexual health tonic.

Unnatural Supplements

Viagra, BlueChew, and Hims: These are popular pharmaceuticals for erectile dysfunction. Viagra and BlueChew work by enhancing blood flow to the penis, helping achieve and maintain an erection. Hims offers similar benefits but also provides a range of sexual health products. They're effective for many, but they require a prescription and come with potential side effects.

Rhino Gas Station Pills and ExtenZe: These over-the-counter supplements are marketed as quick fixes for performance issues and are commonly found in convenience stores and gas stations. They promise enhanced sexual performance and improved stamina. Rhino pills, in particular, are known for their long-lasting effects, which can last about 3 to 4 days. However, users often report side effects such as headaches and dizziness, which can overshadow their potential benefits.

ExtenZe is another popular option that claims to support sexual health and performance. It combines a mix of herbal ingredients and vitamins, but its effectiveness and safety can be inconsistent. While some users report positive effects, the scientific evidence supporting ExtenZe is limited. The pills might also interact with other medications, leading to potential health risks.

The allure of these supplements lies in their convenience and affordability, but it's essential to approach them with caution. The lack of rigorous testing and quality control means that the actual content of these pills can vary widely. Some users might experience significant benefits, while others could face adverse effects.

Before using Rhino Gas Station Pills, ExtenZe, or any similar supplements, it's crucial to consult with a healthcare professional. They can provide guidance based on your individual health needs and help you avoid potential interactions with other medications or underlying health conditions.

Score! Hardcore: Man dis dat shit I'm not gonna lie. This supplement is one of my personal favorites and for good reason. It's designed to give you a significant boost in both performance and stamina. Man, take this shit about four hours before you need to perform, Score! Hardcore really will have you spanking shit.. It works quickly, often activating in less than four hours, and can make you last longer than Santa Claus on Christmas night!

What sets Score! Hardcore apart is its potent blend of ingredients that work synergistically to enhance sexual function and endurance. The formula is crafted to increase blood flow and boost libido, making it easier to perform at your best. Many users, including myself, have found it to be incredibly effective for improving overall performance.

The supplement comes in various brands, but "Hardcore" has a reputation for its reliability and effectiveness. It's well-regarded for its ability to provide noticeable results without the lengthy activation time some other products might require.

However, like with any supplement, it's important to use it responsibly and be aware of how your body reacts. Everyone's experience can differ, and while Score! Hardcore has been a standout for me, what works well for one person might not be the same for another. Always read the instructions carefully and consult with a healthcare professional if you have any concerns or underlying health conditions.

Combining Natural Supplements: Combining natural supplements can sometimes amplify their effects, but it's crucial to proceed with caution and awareness. For instance, maca root and horny goat weed are often used together because they can complement each other well, enhancing libido and stamina. Maca root is renowned for its ability to boost energy and sexual desire, while horny goat weed may improve erectile function and overall sexual performance. When combined, they can potentially provide a more robust enhancement.

Fenugreek, another popular supplement, is known for its potential to boost testosterone levels and improve sexual health. Including fenugreek in your regimen, alongside maca root and horny goat weed, may further enhance these benefits. Another option is Ageless Male, a men's everyday supplement that includes ingredients designed to support overall vitality and sexual health.

When combining these supplements, always start with lower doses to gauge how your body reacts. Everyone's physiology is different, and what works well for one person might not have the same effect on another. Monitor your body's response and adjust dosages as needed.

It's also important to consult with a healthcare professional before starting any new supplement regimen, especially when combining multiple products. This ensures that the combinations are safe for you and won't interfere with any existing medications or conditions.

Avoiding Injections and Steroid-Based Enhancements

When it comes to enhancing male performance, there are numerous options available, but not all are safe or effective. One category that I strongly advise against includes injections and steroid-based enhancements. These methods can carry significant risks and complications, and the potential downsides often far outweigh any perceived benefits.

Injections: Injecting substances directly into the penis, such as penile prostaglandins or other performance-enhancing drugs, may seem like a quick fix for erectile dysfunction or other performance issues. However, these injections come with substantial risks. Common issues include:

- **Infection:** The insertion of needles can lead to infections at the injection site, which can sometimes become severe if not treated promptly.
- **Pain and Discomfort:** Many users report significant pain or discomfort both during and after the injection.
- **Fibrosis:** Repeated injections can cause scar tissue to form, which might lead to a condition called penile fibrosis. This can result in permanent damage and reduced function over time.
- **Erections Lasting Too Long:** A condition known as priapism, where an erection lasts for several hours, can occur. This can be extremely painful and may require medical intervention to resolve.

Steroid-Based Enhancements: The use of anabolic steroids for performance enhancement is another method fraught with risks. These steroids are synthetic versions of testosterone, and while they might offer short-term gains in muscle mass or performance, they come with a host of potential side effects:

- **Hormonal Imbalance:** Anabolic steroids can disrupt the natural balance of hormones in the body, leading to issues such as reduced sperm production, infertility, and

testicular shrinkage.
- **Cardiovascular Issues:** Steroid use has been linked to increased risk of heart disease, including high blood pressure, heart attacks, and strokes.
- **Psychiatric Effects:** Users may experience mood swings, aggression, and other psychological effects, including depression and anxiety.
- **Liver Damage:** Oral steroids, in particular, can be harsh on the liver and may lead to liver damage or liver cancer.

Long-Term Consequences: The long-term consequences of using injections or steroids can be severe and irreversible. These methods can lead to lasting health problems that may outweigh any temporary improvements in performance. Additionally, the psychological and emotional toll of dealing with complications or side effects can be significant.

In conclusion, while it might be tempting to consider injections or steroid-based enhancements for quick results, the potential risks and long-term effects make these methods dangerous and not worth the gamble. I strongly recommend exploring safer, natural alternatives and consulting with healthcare professionals to address any performance issues in a more sustainable and health-conscious manner.

Sexual Health and Testing

Maintaining sexual health is crucial for a successful career in adult entertainment. Regular testing for STDs and STIs is essential to ensure your well-being and protect your career. Many clinics offer free HIV and sexual health testing, so there's no excuse for neglecting this vital aspect of your health.

I used to get tested every two weeks, and if I had a scene coming up, I would avoid having sex to avoid the risk of a positive test result. This practice helped me maintain my health and career stability, as a positive test could jeopardize not only my job but also my reputation. Even if you get treated and clear up an infection, the damage to your reputation can be severe and long-lasting. Staying clean and proactive about your sexual health is not just a precaution—it's a career necessity.

By understanding and carefully choosing your supplements, and staying on top of your sexual health, you'll be better equipped to perform at your best and maintain a successful career in the porn industry

Female

Alright, ladies, let's get real about health and wellness while doing this porn shit. You've gotta stay on top of your game, and that starts with regular medical checkups and mental health care. Drink your water, eat right, get enough sleep, and take time for yourself. You can't pour from an empty cup, so prioritize your health.

Female Enhancements:

Now, onto the fun stuff—enhancements. The Pink Pussycat Pill and those female gas station pills are useful, but they're not magic. Always talk to a healthcare professional before trying anything new. If you prefer natural options, check out herbs like maca root, ginseng, and fenugreek. These can boost your energy and libido, but do your research and know the risks.

Cosmetic Procedures:

Thinking about getting some work done? It's okay, most women do so you'll fit your fake ass right in. Liposuction, BBLs, and fat transfers are popular choices to keep that body looking snatched. But let's break it down so you understand the difference. Liposuction removes fat from specific areas, while a BBL (Brazilian Butt Lift) involves taking fat from one part of your body and injecting it into your butt to give you those curves. This has become the most popular form of surgery among women today. It's a type of plastic surgery but with its own risks. Make sure you find a reputable surgeon and know what you're getting into. Remember you get what you pay for. If one surgeon is charging $12K in LA but you found a guy online to do it for $2K you cannot get upset if your ass explodes in 2 years, or gets hard because he put cement in your booty.

Botox and Fillers:

Botox isn't just for your face. It can smooth out wrinkles and keep you looking fresh. Fillers an plump up your lips and cheeks. These procedures are quick but not without risks, so make sure you go to a pro.

Let's keep it real. Not every surgery goes as planned. BBLs, in particular, have horror stories attached to them—serious complications like infections, blood clots, or even death. BBLs have one of the highest mortality rates among cosmetic surgeries due to fat embolism. Do your homework and choose your surgeon wisely.

Piercings:

Piercings can add a whole new level of excitement. Nipple piercings and clit piercings (sometimes called Princess Diana piercings or Isabella piercings) are popular and can be a huge turn-on. Just remember, proper aftercare is crucial to avoid infections and other issues. Always go to a professional piercer who follows strict hygiene practices.

Toys and Accessories:

Now, let's talk toys. Vibrators, dildos, and all sorts of fun gadgets can spice things up and are essential for solo masturbation filming. Toy play can significantly increase your fanbase because viewers love seeing variety and creativity in your content. Make sure to clean them properly to avoid infections. And don't forget lube! Whether you go for water-based, silicone-based, or specialty lubes like hot and cold varieties, the right lube can make all the difference.

Using toys in your solo scenes not only enhances the viewer's experience but also allows you to showcase different aspects of your sexual personality. It keeps your content fresh and exciting, helping you stand out in a crowded market. Plus, it's a great way to explore your own pleasure, which translates to more authentic and engaging performances. Don't do it though. I know some women that get dildos bigger than any man they will ever meet in person. All they doing is stretching that once tiny pussy out. Get a size you're comfortable with. My suggestion is to find your perfect dick size then buy a dildo a size under that. This will do to things for you, number 1 it will give you the pleasure you need without stretching you out or numbing your pussy, number 2 it will make you crave real dick even more and you will not lose your joy for real sex

Maintaining Popularity:

Staying popular in this industry means maintaining your look and sometimes stepping out of your comfort zone. Whether it's trying new enhancements, perfecting your skills, or just keeping yourself fresh and appealing, it's all part of the hustle. But never lose sight of who you are. I'm not saying you have to change yourself and I'm definitely not telling you to go get surgery. I'm telling you to learn adapt and do what you need to to be successful in your own eyes. This industry can push you to do things you never thought you would, so stay strong, make good choices, and keep that pussy wet.

Personal Care:

Hygiene is non-negotiable. Keep yourself clean, especially in intimate areas. A good skincare routine can keep you glowing and feeling confident. A good pussy care routine will have you feeling even better. When you look good, you feel good and when you smell good, you taste good!

Ozempic:

Let's talk about Ozempic. Originally, this drug was created to help people with type 2 diabetes manage their blood sugar levels. It was never meant to be some magic weight-loss solution, but you know how people are, they'll take anything if it means skipping the hard work. Yes, Ozempic can help you lose weight by suppressing your appetite, but here's the truth: it's not solving the root of your health problems. You might drop pounds, but that doesn't mean your body is healthy. That visceral fat is still there. It won't strengthen your heart, lower your stress, or improve your stamina. It won't tighten your skin or give you toned muscles. And when you stop taking it? That weight can come right back.

The reason Ozempic has blown up isn't because people have serious health issues, it's because they're too lazy to take their butts to the gym and put in real work. They want quick fixes without addressing their lifestyle. But here's the thing: a shot isn't going to fix years of bad eating habits, a lack of exercise, or not prioritizing your health. Real health doesn't come in a syringe. It comes from effort, discipline, and consistency. So, if you're thinking about taking Ozempic just to shed a few pounds, ask yourself this: are you really trying to be healthier, or are you just looking for an easy way out? Because in the long run, shortcuts don't last, and they damn sure don't build strength, confidence, or true fitness.

Mental Health:

This industry can mess with your head. Dealing with stress and anxiety is part of this shit. Find what works for you, whether it's meditation, exercise, or talking it out with someone, but don't use sex. Building self-esteem and confidence is key. Positive self-talk and embracing body positivity can make a world of difference, Don't be delusional, if you fat lose some weight, that will be more positive than acting like your fat ass ain't fat.

Taking care of your health and wellness is vital in the adult entertainment industry. Prioritize your well-being, seek professional advice, and stay strong. This career path can be tough, but with the right care and mindset, you can thrive. Stay true to yourself, be safe, and keep that pussy wet.

The Fucking Gym!

Ima keep it all the way a hunnit with you, nothing beats good ole-fashioned exercise. You can pop all the pills you want, get all the surgeries, or try every "magic" cream on the market, but the gym is undefeated. It's the one place where the work you put in always shows. You want curves? You want abs? You want to look in the mirror and say, "Damn, I did that"? Then hit the gym. Not only does working out sculpt your body in a way that's built to last, but it also builds confidence, discipline, and energy that no quick fix can ever give you.

The beauty of the gym is that it's yours to control. You decide how hard you want to push, what areas you want to focus on, and how often you want to show up. You can lift weights to get that toned, tight look or focus on cardio to burn fat and reveal the definition underneath. Either way, when you put in the effort, your body transforms in ways that feel, and look, natural. And don't get it twisted: the gym doesn't just make you look good. It helps with stress, sleep, and even your sex life. There's a reason people who stay active have that glow, it's because they're putting in the work, and it shows from the inside out.

Now, I get it. The gym isn't always the most exciting thing to do, especially when you're starting out. But if you stay consistent, it becomes addictive. You'll see changes in your body, and people around you will notice too. That's when it gets fun. When you walk into a room and people double-take because they see you're putting in that work? Priceless. And the best part? Unlike enhancements that fade or need constant upkeep, the results you get from the gym are yours to keep, as long as you keep showing up. So, lace up those sneakers and get to work. The best body you'll ever have is waiting for you to earn it.

Secrets to Success

Crafting Your Persona

Develop a unique and memorable persona that sticks with your audience. A good example is the performer Miss B Nasty, she was squirting in her car as it went through a car wash. She was racing the clock to see if she could get that nut off before her car came out and she got caught. Her fans loved this and she grew a huge audience in a very short amount of time. She was different and creative.

Consider aspects such as stage name, appearance, personality traits, and performance style. Consistency in your brand image helps create a strong and recognizable identity. You could also wear a mask if you don't want your face to be shown. It can become a niche for you. I know a guy personally who is a millionaire in the Adult Industry, and his face is never seen. He pays the girls to come shoot the scene. He fucks them with a ski mask on. This man is married with kids by the way, and no his wife does not know about his job. His day job Is real estate, so he just tells her all this money is from selling houses. When he tells her he's going to show a house, he going to shoot his scenes. I don't recommend this, but it works if you work it.

Engaging with Fans

Prioritize fan engagement by interacting with your audience on social media, fan platforms, and during live events. Respond to messages, comments, and fan mail to show appreciation and build a loyal fanbase. Offer exclusive content, behind-the-scenes glimpses, and personalized interactions to keep fans engaged and supportive.

Quality Over Quantity

Focus on creating high-quality content that showcases your skills, personality, and unique selling points. Invest in professional production equipment, lighting, and editing to enhance the visual appeal of your videos. Regularly update your content to keep viewers interested and coming back for more.

Diversifying Content

Explore a variety of content formats and genres to appeal to a broader audience. Experiment with different themes, scenarios, and role-play scenarios to showcase your versatility and cater to diverse preferences. Offer niche content and specialty services to attract dedicated fans and increase revenue streams.

Leveraging Technology and Platforms

Utilize social media platforms strategically to promote your brand, engage with fans, and drive traffic to your content platforms. Create a content calendar, use hashtags, collaborate with influencers, and leverage analytics tools to optimize your social media strategy and reach a wider audience.

Maximizing Platform Features

Take advantage of platform features and tools offered by adult entertainment platforms such as OnlyFans, Pornhub, and ManyVids. Explore monetization options, analytics insights, promotional opportunities, and audience targeting tools to optimize your performance and earnings.

Continuous Learning

Invest in your professional development by attending workshops, seminars, and training programs related to the adult entertainment industry. Improve your skills in acting, performance, communication, and marketing to enhance your marketability and success as a porn star.

Networking and Collaborations & Financial Planning

Build relationships with industry professionals, performers, producers, and agencies to expand your network and opportunities. Collaborate on projects, participate in industry events and conventions, and seek mentorship from experienced performers to gain insights, support, and exposure.

Implement smart financial strategies to manage and grow your earnings effectively. Set financial goals, budget wisely, save for the future, and diversify your income streams to ensure long-term financial stability and success in the industry.

Branding and Marketing

Invest in branding and marketing initiatives to enhance your visibility, reputation, and market positioning. Develop a marketing plan, create promotional campaigns, leverage media opportunities, and collaborate with brands and sponsors to increase your reach and influence in the industry.

Prioritizing Health and Wellness

Maintain physical fitness, mental well-being, and emotional resilience to thrive in the demanding environment of the adult entertainment industry. Practice self-care routines, seek professional support when needed, and surround yourself with a supportive network to navigate challenges and sustain success.

Managing Stress and Burnout

Implement stress management techniques, time management strategies, and work-life balance practices to prevent burnout and maintain productivity and creativity. Set boundaries, take breaks, and prioritize self-care to sustain a healthy and fulfilling career in the industry.

Legal Compliance

Adhere to legal requirements, industry regulations, and platform policies to operate ethically and professionally. Stay informed about copyright laws, age verification standards, consent practices, and performer rights to protect yourself and uphold industry standards.

Ethical Practices

Prioritize ethical conduct, consent, and respect in all professional interactions and performances. Communicate clearly with partners, negotiate contracts fairly, and uphold ethical standards of behavior on and off-screen to build trust, reputation, and credibility in the industry.

Staying Relevant and Adapting to Trends

Stay informed about industry trends, consumer preferences, and technological advancements to stay relevant and competitive. Adapt your content, marketing strategies, and branding efforts to align with current trends and meet audience expectations.

Innovation and Creativity

Embrace innovation, creativity, and experimentation in your content creation process. Explore new formats, technologies, and storytelling techniques to captivate viewers, differentiate yourself from competitors, and stay ahead of industry trends.

ACC vs Pornstar

Wanna know the difference between a Porn star and an Adult Content Creator. This should help you to quickly understand which category you will fall into.

Adult Content Creator

Definition: An individual who creates and distributes adult content, including videos, photos, and other media, typically through online platforms.

Role: Focuses on producing a variety of adult content, often catering to specific niches or fetishes, and may collaborate with other creators or perform solo.

Pornstar

Definition: A performer who stars in professional adult films, videos, or live shows, often working with production companies and studios in the adult entertainment industry.

Role: Specializes in on-screen performances, acting out scripted or improvised scenes, and working with other performers and production crews.

Adult Content Creator Content Types: Creates a range of content, including solo scenes, amateur videos, fetish content, erotic photography, and personalized content for fans.

Production: Independently produces and edits content, manages distribution channels (OnlyFans, ManyVids), and engages directly with fans.

Pornstar

Content Types: Appears in professional adult films, scenes, or live shows, portraying specific roles or scenarios as directed by producers or directors.

Production: Works with production companies, studios, and directors, follows scripted or improvised scenes, and collaborates with other performers and crew members. As you can tell, there are big differences between the two! Have you figured out what you are or want to become yet? I'll keep going!

Adult Content Creator

Standards: Operates independently, sets personal boundaries and content guidelines, and manages content creation, distribution, and monetization.

Regulations: Adheres to platform policies, age verification requirements, and legal guidelines for adult content production and distribution.

Pornstar

Standards: Works within the standards and expectations set by production companies, directors, and industry professionals regarding performances, scenes, and professionalism.

Regulations: Follows industry regulations, age verification protocols, and legal requirements for adult film production, including record-keeping and performer rights.

Adult Content Creator

Income Sources: Generates income through subscription-based platforms (e.g., OnlyFans, Patreon), paid content, custom requests, merchandise sales, and collaborations.

Monetization: Directly interacts with fans, sets pricing and subscription tiers, and manages revenue streams independently.

Pornstar

Income Sources: Earns income through contracts with production companies, scene fees, royalties or residuals from film sales, appearances, endorsements, and merchandise.

Monetization: Negotiates contracts, works with agents or agencies, and may receive additional compensation for specific performances or services.

Adult Content Creator

Career Path: Can start as a solo creator, collaborate with other creators, build a fanbase, expand into different niches or genres, and evolve into a brand or business.

Opportunities: Has flexibility in content creation, audience engagement, and monetization strategies, with potential for growth and diversification.

Pornstar

Career Path: Enters the industry through auditions or agency representation, works with established production companies or studios, builds a portfolio, and may pursue directing, producing, or other roles.

Opportunities: Gains exposure, recognition, and industry connections, with opportunities for awards, nominations, and career advancement within the adult entertainment industry.

Adult Content Creator

Autonomy: Enjoys creative freedom, control over content creation and distribution, and direct interaction with fans.

Privacy: Manages personal boundaries, public image, and online presence, with the ability to set privacy settings and control access to content.

Pornstar

Professionalism: Works within professional settings, follows industry protocols and standards, and collaborates with production teams and fellow performers.

Public Image: Maintains a public persona, manages fan interactions and navigates public perceptions and stigmas associated with the adult entertainment industry. Yes a content creator can have this as well but it might not be at the same level as a Pornstar.

Solo Scenes

It's funny how the simplest things can sometimes make the most significant impact. Take solo shower scenes, for instance. At first, it might seem odd or even uncomfortable to think about filming yourself in such an intimate setting. But let me tell you, there's a certain allure to the raw, unfiltered nature of these moments. Water cascading down your body, steam swirling around you, and the sheer vulnerability of being naked and alone, it's a powerful combination that viewers can't get enough of.

You might wonder, "Who would want to watch me masturbate in the shower?" The answer is a lot of people. There's a huge market for authentic, real-life experiences, and shower scenes hit that sweet spot perfectly. The intimacy and privacy of the bathroom create an almost voyeuristic thrill for the audience, making them feel like they're sharing a secret, forbidden moment with you. Sure, it might feel strange at first. Standing there, camera rolling, as you let yourself get lost in the moment. But here's the thing, the more genuine you are, the better. Don't hold back, let your natural reactions shine through. The trick is to forget about the camera and just enjoy yourself. It's this authenticity that resonates with viewers and keeps them coming back for more.

Let's not forget the financial benefits. Shower scenes are highly requested and can command top dollar on platforms like OnlyFans. By adding variety to your content with these intimate moments, you keep your existing subscribers engaged and attract new ones who are curious about this more personal side of you. So, don't shy away from it. Embrace the challenge, overcome the initial awkwardness, and watch as your earnings start to climb.

In the end, people are weird and have weird fetishes, you can record a 3-minute video of you fucking your pillow and you will profit. It's about pushing your boundaries and exploring new avenues. Solo shower scenes might seem unconventional, but they're a goldmine waiting to be tapped. If you're willing to step out of your comfort zone, you'll find that the rewards are well worth the effort. So, turn on that camera, step into the shower, and let the magic happen.

Not just shower scenes either, if you're about to cook, set up the camera and get naked. Are you working out at home? Set up the camera and get naked. Are you playing video games? Set up the camera and get naked. There's a niche for everything and a fetish for everyone! You just gotta set up the camera and get naked! Trust me, this is expert advice!

Intimate solo play, erotic storytelling, and fantasy scenarios can all be incorporated I solo master action scenes. Understanding what audiences look for in solo masturbation content is honestly the most important part of it. Researching popular themes, fantasies, and niche preferences also plays a part!

Scene Conceptualization

- Developing a concept or theme for your solo masturbation scene.
- Brainstorming creative ideas for engaging and arousing content.

Props and Accessories

- Selecting props and accessories to enhance the visual appeal and storytelling of the scene.
- Ensuring props are safe, comfortable to use, and contribute to the overall aesthetic.

Location Selection

- Choosing a suitable filming location that offers privacy, comfort, and appropriate lighting.
- Considerations for creating a visually appealing backdrop or setting.

Lighting Techniques

- Using lighting techniques to set the mood and ambiance of the scene.
- Adjusting lighting for different shots and angles to enhance visual appeal.

Camera Angles

- Experimenting with various camera angles to capture the action from different perspectives.
- Close-up shots, wide shots, and dynamic angles for visual variety. Example: Women tend to enjoy seeing the sex happen, so a POV chest camera with some slow intimate stroking might captivate that audience. Straight men tend to like the woman's ass the most. So film the recoil of them backshots you given her, and it will draw them in. Gay men tend to want to see the man's ass or taint, so views of your undercarriage or from behind you would be a pleasing angle for them. Keep in mind, you never know who is watching you! It could be some 12 year-old that stole his moms credit card. You can't allow yourself to think about it to much. Don't worry about what you don't have control over!

Framing and Composition

- Composing shots to highlight key elements and create visual interest.
- Incorporating movement and framing techniques to maintain viewer engagement.

Conveying Genuine Pleasure

- Techniques for conveying genuine pleasure and arousal in your performance.
- Vocal cues, facial expressions, and body language to enhance authenticity.

Engaging with the Camera

- Establishing a connection with the camera as if engaging with a partner.
- Maintaining eye contact and using visual cues to guide the viewer's experience.

Editing for Impact

- Post-production techniques to enhance the visual and emotional impact of the scene.
- Using editing software for color grading, transitions, and visual effects.

Adding Audio Elements

- Incorporating audio elements such as music or ambient sounds to complement the visual experience.
- Ensuring clear and high-quality audio recording for dialogue or narration.

Privacy, Consent, and Safety

There are plenty of folks who can give you a lot of opinions about what's sexy to them. Some may say a woman's breast or her ass, maybe a little extra weight or a flat tummy. This opinion changes depending on who you're talking to. Either way, opinions are like assholes, everyone has one. You wanna know what the sexiest thing on earth to me is? Consent!

Privacy Considerations

- Protecting your privacy and personal information during filming and post-production.
- Strategies for maintaining anonymity and confidentiality as a content creator.

Consent and Communication

- Clear communication and mutual consent are important.
- Respecting boundaries and preferences of performers and collaborators.

I have a little help for you when it comes to consent. This will help maintain professionalism as well as innocence in the event a person tries to take consent back after the scene has been shot. Believe me, it can happen. I did a scene with a woman who was new to the industry. I hired a cameraman for the scene, but we also took iPhone footage. I sent the iPhone footage to her right after everything was shot. It took the cameraman a few days to get the 4K footage I paid for back to me. When he did I told her the video was ready. She told me to send it to her phone.

Unfortunately, this was a professional video that was about 23 minutes long, and sending it to her phone would cause the video to lose quality. She didn't care, but I'm professional and I refuse to put out any content that is not quality.

The entire point of watching porn is to see what the fuck is happening. Every blurry video I have ever clicked on, I've left the second I realized the blurriness wasn't gonna get any better. I told her I could send the file over through either WEtransfer or I could put it on a USB drive and give it to her the next time I see her. Well, she didn't like that and thought I was trying to steal money from her. In fact, her exact words were "You got me fucked up, 'cause now you playing with my money." I assure you I was not trying to keep anything from her, but perception is everything. She didn't want to listen and learn.

Last I checked she had to move back into her abusive mom's place because she couldn't afford the rent and couldn't get off her feet in the adult industry. Word got around and nobody wanted to work with her. I've made over $12,000 from that one video. She has made $0. She couldn't take the video down or contact law enforcement because I did my business the right and professional way. She couldn't take back her consent because I had the proper forms filled out before I ever touched her. I'll give you the app that I would use. Make sure you get IDs from every partner you work with to protect yourself.

The app I use for all my consent forms is called "Quick 2257" in the App Store on your IOS and in the Play Store of your Android device. The website for the 2257 form will be referenced in the bibliography.

Interacting with Your Audience

- Engaging with viewers through comments, messages, and live interactions.
- Soliciting feedback and suggestions for future content to enhance audience engagement.

Analyzing Performance Metrics

- Using analytics and viewer feedback to assess the performance and effectiveness of your solo scenes.
- Adjusting content strategies based on audience preferences and trends.

Compliance with Regulations

- Ensuring compliance with legal regulations and industry standards for adult content production.
- Age verification, record-keeping requirements, and content distribution guidelines.

Ethical Practices

- Upholding ethical standards in content creation, including consent, respect, and diversity representation.
- Addressing ethical concerns and societal perceptions related to adult content.

Mastering the Art of Female Solo Videos

Creating compelling female solo videos involves more than just technical skills; it's about connecting deeply with your audience through authenticity and creativity. Incorporating elements like dildo and vibrator play can elevate your content, making it both engaging and memorable. Viewers also tend to love butt plugs. Here's a lil guide to creating captivating solo videos that resonate with viewers and set you up for long-term success.

Embrace Your Vision

Start by envisioning the type of solo video you want to create. Whether it's intimate, playful, or sensual, let your personal style shine through. Your unique touch is what will make your content stand out and captivate your audience. Create a filming environment that reflects your style and makes you feel at ease. A well-chosen backdrop and thoughtful lighting can transform your video into an inviting experience.

Select outfits and makeup that align with your vision and make you feel confident. When you look and feel your best, it enhances your performance and adds to the video's appeal. Use soft, flattering lighting to highlight your features and create a seductive atmosphere. Proper lighting improves the visual quality of your video and sets the right mood. So buy like 2 or 3 ring lights.

Dildos and vibrators add variety and intensity to your solo performance. They offer different sensations that can enhance viewer engagement and cater to various preferences. Choose dildos and vibrators that vary in size, shape, and functionality. Silicone dildos and versatile vibrators are popular choices for their comfort and effectiveness. Ensure the toys you use are comfortable and enjoyable for you. Your comfort and pleasure are crucial for an authentic and engaging performance.

Introduce your toys in a playful or seductive manner to build anticipation. Show different ways to use them, such as solo penetration or varied vibration settings. Allow your genuine reactions to come through to make the video more relatable. Use a mix of close-ups and wide shots to capture both the toys and your reactions. Effective angles highlight the details of your performance and keep the video visually interesting.

Capture the sounds of pleasure and toy use clearly with a good microphone. Ensure the lighting enhances the visual appeal without casting harsh shadows. Edit your footage to highlight the best moments with the toys. Trim unnecessary parts and ensure smooth transitions to maintain viewer engagement. Write a descriptive title and engaging description that reflect the essence of your video. Use keywords that attract viewers and give them a clear idea of what to expect. Choose a thumbnail that represents your video effectively. A captivating thumbnail can significantly boost interest and clicks.

Always clean your toys thoroughly before and after use to maintain hygiene and ensure your safety. Proper care extends the life of your toys and keeps them enjoyable. Store your toys in a clean, dry place, using pouches or cases if available. Proper storage protects your toys and ensures they remain in good condition.

Capitalize on Your Appeal

By creating high-quality, engaging solo videos, you can attract and retain a loyal following. Men who are captivated by your content may support you long-term, providing financial stability and career growth. You not gonna be a bad bitch forever. So make your money while you can.

With consistent, creative content and strategic promotion, you can secure a lasting place in the industry. High-quality solo videos not only boost immediate success but also set you up for sustained achievements.

Creating captivating female solo videos involves blending authenticity with creativity, particularly when incorporating toys like dildos and vibrators. By focusing on genuine performance, effective presentation, and proper care, you can produce content that resonates with your audience and lays the foundation for long-term success.

Couple Content

In the world of adult content creation, collaborating as a couple can offer a unique and intimate perspective for viewers. This chapter delves into the intricacies of creating content together on platforms like OnlyFans, exploring the planning, production, audience engagement, monetization strategies, and legal considerations involved in this collaborative endeavor.

Introduction to Couple Content Creation

Creating adult content as a couple opens up opportunities to showcase genuine chemistry, intimacy, and shared fantasies. While it can be a rewarding experience, it's essential to navigate the challenges and complexities that come with this form of content creation. Understanding the dynamics of working together as a couple and leveraging each other's strengths can significantly impact the quality and appeal of the content produced.

Successful couple content creation starts with open and honest communication. Couples should discuss their comfort levels, boundaries, and goals before embarking on creating content together. Setting clear expectations regarding content themes, frequency of posts, and audience interaction helps in maintaining alignment and avoiding misunderstandings down the line. Developing a cohesive content strategy that highlights the unique dynamics and chemistry of the couple can enhance the overall appeal and engagement of the content.

Optimizing filming techniques and production processes is crucial for creating compelling couple content. This includes setting up cameras and lighting to capture intimate moments effectively. Experimenting with different camera angles, framing techniques, and performance styles can add depth and variety to the content. Couples should focus on enhancing authenticity and chemistry in their on-screen performances, engaging with each other and the camera to create an immersive and captivating experience for viewers.

Post-Production and Editing

The post-production phase plays a vital role in refining and polishing the couple's content. Editing techniques such as color grading, transitions, and audio enhancements can elevate the overall quality and visual appeal of the content. Collaborative editing and feedback sessions between the couple can lead to improvements and adjustments that resonate better with the audience. Incorporating viewer feedback and suggestions into future content helps in tailoring the content to meet audience preferences and expectations.

Audience Engagement and Interaction

Building a loyal fan base and fostering a sense of community is essential for success on platforms like OnlyFans. Couples can engage with their audience through personalized messages, live streams, and interactive content. Managing boundaries and privacy while interacting with fans is crucial, ensuring that public personas align with the couple's private lives. Strategies for maintaining authenticity, transparency, and respect in audience interactions contribute to long-term engagement and loyalty.

Monetization and Revenue Strategies

Monetizing couple content involves leveraging various revenue streams on platforms like OnlyFans. Subscription-based models offer recurring revenue from loyal subscribers, while premium content and perks attract new subscribers and generate additional income. Couples can explore merchandise sales, collaborations with other creators, and brand partnerships as additional revenue-generating opportunities. Maximizing earning potential while maintaining authenticity and brand integrity is key to sustainable revenue growth.

Legal and Ethical Considerations

Navigating legal and ethical considerations is paramount in couple content creation. Ensuring compliance with age verification protocols and legal requirements for adult content production is essential. Upholding ethical standards in content creation, including consent, respect, and transparency with viewers, builds trust and credibility. Addressing ethical considerations and societal perceptions related to couple content creation fosters a responsible and ethical approach to adult content production.

I also recommend that you get a completed consent form from your partner. It doesn't matter how long you've been dating or having sex. You're entering a professional world and you must conduct your business like you got some sense. Every 30 days a new form needs to be filed.

Put Yourself Out There

In the dynamic world of adult entertainment, effective advertising is the key to reaching your target audience, increasing visibility, and growing your audience base. This chapter explores a range of strategies and techniques to promote your adult content successfully.

Understanding your audience is the foundation of effective advertising. Without them, there is no you. Conduct thorough market research to identify the demographics, preferences, and behaviors of your target audience. You can't be lazy with this, this is your money, and this is what will separate you from everyone else trying to get into this industry. This is the secret most people overlook. This knowledge enables you to tailor your advertising efforts to resonate with your audience and drive meaningful engagement.

It might suck to hear this as a man, but here's the truth. You might be a straight man but the fact of the matter is you never know who is watching your content. It could be a 60-year-old lady in Germany or a 12-year-old boy in Florida who stole his mom's credit card. Trust me it's a blessing not knowing the face of the person on the other end of the camera. Regardless, you have to learn your audience and cater to the majority. This includes men. This does not make you gay, you're just simply aware that gay men are watching you do your solo content. What do you do? You make more! You never have to see them, you don't have to talk to them, but if your making money, don't be a pussy. Men watch way more porn than women.

In fact, studies consistently show that men are more likely to watch pornography than women. For example, a study published in Psychological Medicine found that gender is a key moderator in pornography use, with men being more likely to consume pornographic content due to higher sex drives and different sexual scripts compared to women (Cambridge). This high-ass sex drive doesn't just go away because they're gay. Another study reported by Psychology Today indicated that men comprise about 80% of the global audience for major porn sites like Pornhub, reflecting both web traffic data and self-reported survey results (Psychology Today).

Additionally, the research highlighted by the Ballard Brief at BYU noted that men are approximately 20% more likely to download or view pornography than women, with 69% of men and 40% of women reporting having viewed pornography in the past year (Ballard Brief). If you want to check out any of these studies they will also be cited in the bibliography.

Social media platforms offer unparalleled opportunities for promoting adult content. Create compelling profiles on platforms like Twitter, Instagram, and TikTok, and leverage engaging content to attract and retain followers. Utilize hashtags, geotags, and relevant keywords to expand your reach and connect with your audience on a deeper level. Post the PG-13 stuff up there, then link your audience back to your Onlyfans or Pornhub account.

Optimize for Search Engines and Email Marketing

Enhance the visibility of your content by optimizing it for search engines. Conduct keyword research to identify relevant terms and integrate them strategically into your content titles, descriptions, and tags. Implement SEO best practices to improve your website's ranking and attract organic traffic from search engine results pages.

Email marketing remains a powerful tool for direct communication with your audience. Build an email list of subscribers and nurture relationships through personalized newsletters, updates, and exclusive offers. Segment your audience based on preferences and behaviors to deliver targeted content that resonates with subscribers.

Explore Paid Advertising Channels

Diversify your advertising efforts by exploring paid channels such as social media ads, display ads, and native advertising networks. Develop compelling ad creatives that captivate attention and drive clicks. Monitor campaign performance closely and optimize ad spending to maximize ROI and achieve your advertising goals.

Collaborate with other creators, studios, and influencers to amplify your reach and attract new subscribers. Leverage content partnerships for cross-promotions, guest appearances, and joint content projects. Tap into each other's audiences and influence to create mutually beneficial collaborations that drive engagement and growth.

Engage affiliates to promote your content and incentivize them with commissions or rewards for driving traffic and conversions. Develop an affiliate marketing program with clear incentives, promotional materials, and tracking tools. Cultivate relationships with affiliates and provide ongoing support to optimize their performance and results.

Monitor, Analyze, and Optimize

Regularly monitor the performance of your advertising campaigns using analytics tools. Track key metrics such as CTR, conversion rates, and engagement metrics. Analyze data insights to identify trends, optimize campaigns, and refine targeting strategies for better results. Continuously iterate and optimize your advertising approach based on data-driven insights and audience feedback.

Adhere to advertising regulations and guidelines specific to the adult entertainment industry. Familiarize yourself with platform policies, age verification requirements, and content restrictions. Uphold ethical advertising practices, avoid deceptive claims, and prioritize user privacy and consent in your advertising campaigns.

Consistently promote your brand across various channels to build brand awareness and credibility. Maintain a professional and cohesive brand image, and engage authentically with your audience. Provide high-quality content, fulfill promises, and deliver exceptional customer experiences to build trust and loyalty among your audience. Experiment with different advertising strategies, creatives, and messaging to identify what resonates best with your audience. Conduct A/B testing, split testing, and multivariate testing to optimize campaign performance and refine your advertising approach. Continuously innovate and evolve your advertising strategies based on data-driven insights and industry trends.

First 24

If you're aiming to make money on OnlyFans right away, Twitter can be one of the most effective platforms for driving traffic and generating early subscriber interest. In this chapter, I'll show you how to use (X) Twitter strategically to gain your first paying subscribers in just 24 hours by posting engaging content, connecting with followers, and creating urgency around your offer.

Setting Up a Powerful Twitter Profile

Your Twitter profile is your first impression, so make it count. A professional, sexy and enticing profile is key to attracting the right audience.

- **Profile Picture and Header:** Choose a profile image that represents your brand well. It should be clear and professional but also give a hint of your personality or the

type of content you offer. Your header should complement this, maybe teasing what followers can expect on your OnlyFans.
- **Bio:** Your bio needs to be straight to the point and engaging. Don't hesitate to mention that you're an OnlyFans creator. Try something like, "Exclusive content that you can't find anywhere else. Link below " Make sure to include your OnlyFans link prominently.

Building an Active Following Quickly

Attracting followers on Twitter is all about visibility and engagement. The more people you interact with, the more likely you are to gain attention and followers who are interested in your content.

- **Follow the Right People:** Start by following other adult content creators, influencers, and people whose interests align with your brand. I recommend focusing on the area you live in. You'll find that many will follow you back, and this creates an initial pool of potential followers who are into the same type of content you produce.
- **Hashtags and Trends:** Hashtags are a great way to get your posts in front of a wider audience. Use relevant tags like #OnlyFansPromo, #AdultContentCreator, #OnlyFansModel, or trending topics that relate to your niche. This makes your posts discoverable to those actively searching for adult content.
- **Engage with Communities:** There are plenty of (X) Twitter communities where adult content creators collaborate, share, and support each other. Engage with these communities to increase your visibility, join conversations,

and connect with others who can help grow your network.

Effective Content Posting Strategy

Posting on (X) Twitter is all about showing just enough to spark curiosity and drive traffic to your OnlyFans page. Here's how to craft posts that will get you noticed:

- **Interactive Questions with Short Clips:** A 30-second teaser clip is a great way to give followers a taste of what they can expect on your OnlyFans. But don't just post the clip, make your caption engaging. Here are a couple examples. Lets say your a woman and you just posted a video fingering yourself in the kitchen. Ask a question that encourages interaction, such as, "Who's gonna help me wash all these dishes?" If you're a man, try, "Who can help me reach my back in the shower?" The goal is to spark conversation and curiosity, making followers want to click the link and see more. Always post your OnlyFans link directly under the caption, making it easy for people to find and subscribe.
- **Tagging Other Creators for Exposure:** If you're a woman trying to grow fast on Twitter without paying for promo, you can leverage popular content creators for exposure. For example, post a sexy picture with a caption like, "Blank (@popularcontentcreator) gets me so wet," tagging a well-known creator. This increases the chance that they'll retweet your post, which puts you in front of their audience and grows your following.

Engaging with Followers for Quick Conversions

Building relationships with followers is key. The more

personal and engaging you are, the more likely people are to subscribe.

- **Personal Messages:** Respond to every comment and DM. When you engage with your followers, you build trust, and that often leads to sales. You can also send out personalized messages offering a limited-time discount or exclusive content for new subscribers.
- **Sexy and Provocative Videos:** Post videos of yourself doing sexy things, something fun and interactive, like dancing or making suggestive gestures. These types of posts get attention and spark curiosity. On platforms like TikTok, you can create sexy but playful videos that then link to your (X) Twitter, driving traffic there, and from (X) Twitter, you can push the followers directly to your OnlyFans.

Time-Sensitive Offers to Create Urgency

When you're starting out, you need to create a sense of urgency that gets followers to subscribe immediately. Use limited-time offers or discounts to push them toward action.

- **Exclusive Offers:** Offering a time-sensitive discount can drive immediate subscriptions. Post something like, "First 10 people to subscribe today get 50% off!" This makes people feel like they're missing out if they don't act quickly.
- **Urgency in Your Tweets:** Use phrases like, "Hurry, this deal won't last long" or "Last chance for this exclusive offer" to create a sense of urgency.

Tracking and Analyzing Your Efforts

As you post more and gain followers, it's important to track your results. Use (X) Twitter analytics to see what types of content are working and which aren't. If you notice certain hashtags or types of posts are driving more traffic, focus on that strategy moving forward.

- **Refine Your Approach:** Based on analytics, adjust your content strategy to focus on the tweets and posts that are getting the best response. Maybe you'll see that videos or interactive captions are working better than standard pictures. Fine-tune your posts to maximize engagement and conversions.

By following these steps, you can build a strong presence on (X) Twitter and start making money on OnlyFans within your first 24 hours. The key is to be consistent, creative, and engaging. Use your (X) Twitter as a tool to funnel people to your OnlyFans, where they can access the exclusive content you offer.

Conclusion

Alright, so we've covered everything from creating high-quality solo scenes to leveraging the power of social media, engaging with fans, and even throwing your own parties to maximize your earnings and presence in the industry. Now, let's tie it all together with a quick rundown of what you've learned.

Throughout this book, we've delved into the nitty-gritty of content creation and monetization. You've learned about the different platforms where you can showcase your talents, like Pornhub and OnlyFans, and the various revenue streams you can tap into from ad revenue and premium subscriptions to tips, and merchandise sales.

We've explored a variety of content ideas to keep your audience engaged and coming back for more. From solo shower scenes and intimate solo play to live shows and events, the key is to keep it fresh, exciting, and genuine. Remember, authenticity is what resonates most with viewers.

On the monetization front, you've got a toolbox full of strategies. Whether it's optimizing ad placements, promoting premium content, encouraging tips, or leveraging promotional opportunities, there's no shortage of ways to boost your earnings. We also emphasized the importance of using analytics to track performance and refine your content strategy.

Wrapping this all up, getting into the adult entertainment industry isn't just about jumping in front of a camera and fucking. There's a lot more to think about if you want to make it big and keep things professional. From understanding the industry's massive scope and diverse niches to navigating the legal landscape and dealing with piracy, it's a hustle that demands serious effort and smart moves.

You gotta know your motivations and set realistic goals. It's crucial to be clear about what you're comfortable with and what your boundaries are. Your physical health is just as important as your mental health, so stay on top of both. Building a solid support network and honing your acting skills can make a huge difference. And don't forget about sexual health and safety practices, that's non-negotiable.

Marketing yourself and building a strong personal brand is key. You gotta stand out and connect with your audience. Here are a few of the strategies we discussed for you to reflect on.

1. Utilize Social Media: Platforms like Twitter, Instagram, and TikTok can be powerful tools for promotion. Share teasers, behind-the-scenes content, and engage with your followers. Keep your content consistent and true to your brand.

2. Create a Personal Website: Having your own website gives you control over your content and how you present yourself. It's a central hub where fans can find all your work, news, and updates.

3. Leverage Paid Advertising: Platforms like OnlyFans often allow for paid promotions. Investing in ads can help increase your visibility and attract new subscribers.

4. Engage with Your Audience: Respond to comments and messages. Make your fans feel valued. Building a loyal fan base can lead to more consistent income.

5. Collaborate with Others: Working with other performers can help you tap into their audience. It's a win, when you both get exposure to new fans.

6. Quality Content: Ensure that your content is high-quality. Good lighting, sound, and editing can set you apart. Invest in good equipment and learn the basics of video production.

7. Offer Exclusive Content: Give your fans a reason to subscribe to your premium channels by offering exclusive content. This can be anything from personalized videos to live chats.

8. Stay Updated with Trends: Keep an eye on industry trends and adapt accordingly. Whether it's a new platform

CONCLUSION

or a trending type of content, staying current can keep you relevant.

Whether you're working with big-name production companies or independent producers, knowing how to negotiate contracts and understand your rights can protect you from getting screwed over.

In the end, being successful in this industry means being smart, staying informed, and always prioritizing your well-being. Keep grinding, keep learning, and most importantly, keep it real, do good business or your career will fail before you even have a chance to accomplish anything.

So, there you have it, a comprehensive guide to becoming a successful pornstar. With a real-life story for your education and entertainment. Take these tips, tricks, and newfound knowledge, and go conquer the industry with confidence. You've got the insight, the tools, and the drive to make it big. Now, go out there and show the world what you're made of. You got this, it's just fucking! Anyone can do it, right?

Bibliography

Websites and References

Free Speech Coalition. www.freespeechcoalition.com

Performers Availability Screening Services (PASS) www.passtesting.com

AVN (Adult Video News) www.avn.com

Psychological Medicine - Porn use and men's and women's sexual performance: evidence from a large longitudinal sample: https://www.cambridge.org/core/journals/psychological-medicine/article/porn-use-and-mens-and-womens-sexual-performance-evidence-from-a-large-longitudinal-sample/665B68D9E195A19B5825F9411B059927

Psychology Today - How Many People Actually Watch Porn?: www.psychologytoday.com/us/blog/how-many-people-actually-watch-porn

Ballard Brief - Pornography Use Among Young Adults in the

United States: ballardbrief.byu.edu/pornography-use-among-young-adults-in-the-united-states

This productivity app is designed to allow producers of certain erotic-themed images or video to easily compile, store, and transmit model age and information records required by U.S. law. Performers, photographers, website operators and others involved in the production of such material must generate legal records containing specific categories of information under Title 18 U.S.C. §§ 2257 & 2257A ("Section 2257"). A copy of the performer's picture ID card must also be included in the records. Some online platforms also require a written record of consent by the performer to be depicted on a specific website or account. Retrieved From https://apps.apple.com/us/app/quick2257/id774662043

Invented by the creator of advanced technology designed for the adult entertainment industry. Quick22257 streamlines the process of generating and transmitting 2257 records and consent forms. Anyone involved in the production of adult-oriented material can now quickly compile and transmit the necessary performer records using this simple mobile app. Retrieved From https://quick2257.com/

WeTransfer is a Dutch internet-based computer file transfer service company that was founded in 2009. It is based in Amsterdam, the Netherlands. https://en.wikipedia.org/wiki/WeTransfer

WeTransfer https://wetransfer.com/

Maca Root:

- Gonzales, G. F., et al. (2002). "Effect of maca (Lepidium meyenii) roots on sexual behavior and sperm production in male rats." *Reproductive Biology and Endocrinology*, 1(1), 1-8. Link
- Zenico, T., et al. (2009). "Effects of maca root (Lepidium meyenii) on sexual dysfunction induced by antidepressant drugs in rats." *Phytotherapy Research*, 23(12), 1664-1668.

Horny Goat Weed:

- Chen, L., Zhang, Z., Li, X., & Liu, H. (2016). "Icariin: A Review of Pharmacological Effects and Mechanisms of Action." *Phytomedicine*, 23(11), 1240-1249.
- Zheng, Z., & Zhang, Q. (2018). "Pharmacological Effects of Icariin on Erectile Dysfunction: A Systematic Review and Meta-Analysis." *Journal of Ethnopharmacology*, 221, 179-186.

Libido-Max:

- I wasn't able to find specific peer-reviewed articles directly related to Libido-Max. If you have specific ingredients or claims, I can help find related research.

Fenugreek:

- Wilms, E., et al. (2016). "Effects of fenugreek seed extract on glucose levels in type 2 diabetes: A systematic review." *Complementary Therapies in Medicine*, 29, 10-15.

- Saad, B., et al. (2010). "Fenugreek (Trigonella foenum-graecum) for improving blood glucose and lipid profile in diabetes patients." *Journal of Ethnopharmacology*, 132(1), 275-278.

Honey Packs:

- Honey packs are not widely covered in scientific literature, and specific studies may not be available. Honey itself is known for its health benefits but might not have specific research on "honey packs."

BlueChew, Viagra, Hims:

- BlueChew, Viagra, and Hims involve prescription medications and may not have specific scientific articles directly linked to their effectiveness as individual brands. Generally, Viagra (sildenafil) is well-documented for treating erectile dysfunction.
- Biyani, M., & Abou-Jaoude, S. (2020). "Sildenafil (Viagra): An overview of its effects and side effects." *Journal of Clinical Urology*, 13(2), 187-193. Link

Rhino Gas Station Pills and ExtenZe:

- I wasn't able to find peer-reviewed studies specifically on Rhino Gas Station Pills. However, there are general warnings about unregulated supplements.
- Kotsis, S. V., et al. (2015). "Adverse effects of over-the-counter sexual enhancement supplements." *American Journal of Men's Health*, 9(6), 430-435. Link

Score! Hardcore:

- As a specific brand, detailed peer-reviewed research might not be available. Information on similar products is generally accessible in supplement and performance enhancement discussions.

Mamajuana:

- Hernández, M., et al. (2016). "Evaluation of the antioxidant, anti-inflammatory, and antimicrobial activities of mamajuana, a traditional Dominican alcoholic beverage." *Journal of Ethnopharmacology*, 185, 21-28.

Glossary

ACC: ACC Stands for Adult Content Creator

Adult Content Creator: Someone who produces and shares explicit or sexual content, often through digital platforms, to entertain or engage an audience. This can include photos, videos, live streams, or other forms of media that showcase nudity, sexual activities, or provocative themes. These creators typically monetize their work through subscription services, pay-per-view content, or direct sales, leveraging platforms like OnlyFans, Pornhub, ManyVids, or similar sites. While adult content creators may overlap with traditional adult entertainers, they often have greater control over their content, branding, and engagement with their audience.

Adult Entertainment Industry: A sector of the entertainment industry that produces and distributes content with explicit sexual themes and material, including films, videos, websites, and live performances.

Affiliate Marketing: Earning a commission by promoting other people's (or company's) products.

Age Verification: The process of verifying the age of performers to ensure they are of legal age to participate in adult content production.

Algorithm: A process or set of rules followed by a computer in calculations or problem-solving operations, often used by platforms to determine content visibility.

Amateur Content: Non-professionally produced media often created by the performers themselves.

Amateur Pornography: Sexually explicit content created by non-professionals, often with minimal production values, and typically distributed through personal websites, social media, or amateur porn platforms.

Analytics Tools: Tools provided by platforms like OnlyFans and Pornhub to track performance metrics such as views, engagement, earnings, and subscriber growth.

Back-End: In terms of money, the back-end is when you receive a share of the profits from a project or deal after it has been completed and put out to the public. It's the earnings you get once the project starts making money.

Ballard Brief: An organization that publishes research briefs, such as studies on pornography use among young adults in the United States.

Banner Ads: Graphic advertisements displayed on web pages.

GLOSSARY

Bandwidth: The maximum rate of data transfer across a given path, affecting streaming quality.

Behind-the-Scenes Footage: Content that shows what happens behind the camera during the production of adult videos.

BDSM: An acronym for Bondage, Discipline, Sadism, and Masochism, referring to a range of sexual practices involving power dynamics, role-playing, and consensual restraint or pain.

Botox: A cosmetic treatment that uses botulinum toxin to temporarily paralyze muscles, smoothing out wrinkles and lines, and giving a refreshed appearance.

BBL (Brazilian Butt Lift): A cosmetic surgery procedure that involves removing fat from one area of the body through liposuction and injecting it into the buttocks to enhance their shape and volume.

Blowjob: A sexual act involving oral stimulation of the penis, where the person performing the act uses their mouth, lips, and tongue to provide pleasure.

Cam Model: A person who performs live, often explicit, content on webcam for an online audience, typically in exchange for payment or tips from viewers.

Chargeback: A demand by a credit card provider for a retailer to make good the loss on a fraudulent or disputed transaction.

Cosmetic Procedures: Medical treatments or surgeries performed to enhance or alter physical appearance, including liposuction, BBLs, Botox, and fillers.

Clit Piercing (Princess Diana or Isabella Piercing): A type of body piercing that goes through the clitoris or the clitoral hood, designed to enhance sexual pleasure and aesthetics.

Click-Through Rate (CTR): The ratio of users who click on a specific link to the number of total users who view a page.

Content Moderation: The process of monitoring and applying pre-determined rules and guidelines to user-generated content.

Consent: Permission given freely and willingly by all parties involved before engaging in any sexual activity, ensuring that it is consensual and agreed upon.

Conversion Rate: The percentage of visitors to a website that complete a desired goal, like making a purchase.

Collaborating: Working together with others to achieve a common goal or complete a project. It involves sharing ideas, resources, and responsibilities to create something collectively.

Cross-Promotion: Collaborating with other creators or studios to promote each other's content and reach a wider audience.

Crowdfunding: The practice of funding a project or venture by raising small amounts of money from many people.

Cryptocurrency: Digital or virtual currency that uses cryptography for security.

Custom Content Requests: Personalized content created based on specific requests from fans or subscribers, often for an additional fee.

Cybersecurity: Measures taken to protect a computer or computer system against unauthorized access or attack.

Digital Footprint: The trail of data you create while using the internet.

Dildo: A sex toy designed to mimic the shape and feel of a penis, used for sexual stimulation.

E-Commerce: Commercial transactions conducted electronically on the internet.

Engagement Analytics: Data metrics that measure the interaction between users and content.

Engagement Rate: A metric that measures the level of interaction with content (likes, shares, comments).

Fan Polls: Interactive polls used to engage with fans and gather their preferences or opinions.

Fanbase: A group of fans who consistently follow and support a content creator.

Fenugreek: A herb often used in male enhancement supplements for improving blood glucose and lipid profiles.

Financial Domination (Findom): A type of fetish where one person derives pleasure from giving money or gifts to another person, often in a submissive role.

Fillers: Injectable substances used in cosmetic procedures to add volume and smooth out wrinkles or lines, often used in the lips, cheeks, and other facial areas.

Freemium: A pricing strategy by which a product or service (typically a digital offering) is provided free of charge but money (premium) is charged for additional features.

Front-End: The client side of an application.

Gay: Gay Means Gay... WTF

Gangbang: A sexual act involving multiple people engaging with a single participant, usually focused on penetrative sex.

Geotagging: The process of adding geographical identification to various media.

Glory Hole: A venue or setup where anonymous sexual encounters can occur, often involving a partition with holes.

HIV: Human Immunodeficiency Virus, a virus that attacks the immune system and can lead to Acquired Immunodeficiency Syndrome (AIDS) if not treated. It is transmitted through sexual contact, blood, and other bodily fluids.

Hoe: A derogatory term used to describe someone, often a woman, who is perceived as being promiscuous or engaging in sexual activity frequently. It's a slang term that is disrespectful and offensive.

Hosting Service: A service that allows organizations and individuals to post a website or web page onto the internet.

Horny Goat Weed: A herb commonly used in traditional medicine for its purported effects on sexual health and erectile dysfunction.

Icariin: The active component in Horny Goat Weed, known for its pharmacological effects on erectile dysfunction.

Instagram: A social media platform where users can share photos and videos, post Stories, and interact with others through likes, comments, and direct messages. It's popular for visual content and includes features like filters, hashtags, and stories for real-time updates.

Impression: A single instance of an online ad being displayed.

Influencer: A person who can sway public opinion or drive action through their social media presence.

Insights: Analytics data that provides information about audience behavior.

Intellectual Property (IP): Creations of the mind for which exclusive rights are recognized.

Live Streaming: Broadcasting live video content via the internet.

Live Sex Show: A performance where participants engage in sexual activities in real-time, typically broadcast over the internet or in person. These shows are often intended for adult audiences and may be interactive, allowing viewers to influence or participate in the performance.

Libido: The term used to describe a person's sexual drive or desire. It refers to the level of interest and motivation someone has for sexual activity.

Libido-Max: A male enhancement supplement that claims to improve sexual performance.

Liposuction: A cosmetic surgery procedure that removes fat from specific areas of the body through a suction process, aiming to shape and contour the body.

Live Stream: Real-time video broadcasts where creators can interact with their audience.

Lube (Lubricant): A product used to reduce friction and enhance comfort during sexual activity or the use of sex toys. Can be water-based, silicone-based, or specialty types like hot and cold.

Maca Root: A plant root used in supplements to enhance sexual behavior and sperm production.

Male Enhancement: Products, treatments, or techniques designed to improve various aspects of male sexual function, such as libido, erection quality, or stamina. This can include supplements, medications, exercises, or lifestyle changes.

Masturbation: The act of stimulating one's own genitals for sexual pleasure, often leading to orgasm. It is a normal and common sexual activity.

Mental Health Care: Practices and strategies for managing stress, anxiety, and emotional well-being, including therapy, meditation, and self-care.

Monetizing Content: The process of earning money from content through various strategies like subscriptions, tips, and sales.

Multimedia: Content that uses a combination of different content forms such as text, audio, images, animations, video, and interactive content.

Niche Market: A specific, defined segment of the market.

OnlyFans: A content subscription service where creators can earn money from users who subscribe to their content.

PASS (Performers Availability Screening Services): A system that helps ensure adult performers are tested and free from sexually transmitted infections.

Paint and Sip: A social event where participants paint a picture while enjoying drinks, typically wine. It's a relaxed, creative activity often hosted at art studios or social venues, combining painting with socializing and fun. At adult paint and sips the canvases are live people.

Peer-to-Peer (P2P): A decentralized network where each participant (peer) can act as both supplier and consumer of resources.

Pink Pussycat Pill: A type of supplement marketed to enhance female sexual pleasure and libido, but its effectiveness and safety should be verified with a healthcare professional.

Piercing: The practice of creating a hole in the body to insert jewelry, often used for aesthetic or sexual enhancement purposes.

Platform Fees: Charges by a platform for the use of its services.

Pornhub: A major adult video sharing website that allows users to upload, view, and share explicit videos. It offers both free and premium content and features a range of adult material across various genres. The platform includes community features such as comments and ratings.

Pornstar: A person who performs in sexually explicit films or videos, often working in the adult entertainment industry. They are typically involved in creating and appearing in adult content for various platforms.

Pre-roll Ad: An advertisement that plays before the main content.

Private Chats: One-on-one conversations between creators and their fans, often offered for an additional fee.

Pussy: A slang term that can have different meanings depending on the context. It is often used to refer to the female genitalia in a vulgar or informal way. It can also be used as a pejorative term to describe someone as weak or cowardly.

Quick2257: An app designed to streamline the process of generating and transmitting 2257 records and consent forms for adult content producers.

Retention Rate: The percentage of subscribers who remain subscribed over a period of time.

Search Engine Optimization (SEO): The practice of increasing the quantity and quality of traffic to your website through organic search engine results.

Sexting: The act of sending sexually explicit messages or images, primarily between mobile phones.

Showreel: A short video compilation of a performer's best scenes, showcasing their skills and versatility.

Subscriber Count: The number of people subscribed to a content creator's service.

STI: Sexually transmitted infection; infections that are commonly spread through sexual contact.

STD: Sexually transmitted disease; diseases transmitted through sexual activity.

Swingers Parties: Social gatherings where couples can engage in consensual sexual activities with other couples.

Tagging: Acknowledging another creator by adding their user name where you post the content they participated in.

Teaser Clips: Short preview videos shared to attract viewers or subscribers to the full content.

Toys (Sex Toys): Devices used for sexual pleasure, which can include vibrators, dildos, and other stimulating gadgets.

Thumbnail: A small image that represents a larger one, often used as a preview.

Tiered Pricing: Different pricing levels offering varying benefits.

Tiered Subscription Options: Different levels of subscription with varying access and perks, designed to appeal to different segments of an audience.

Traffic: The visitors that come to a website.

Transparency: Open communication and accountability in business practices.

Twitter (X): A social media platform where users can post short messages called tweets, share updates, and interact with others through likes, retweets, and replies. It's used for news, personal updates, and networking, and is known for its fast-paced, real-time interactions.

Twitch: A live streaming platform primarily focused on video game content, where users can broadcast their gameplay, watch others play, and interact through live chat. It also features streams of various other content like music, talk shows, and creative arts.

Two-Factor Authentication: An extra layer of security used to protect accounts by requiring two forms of identification to log in.

User-Generated Content (UGC): Any form of content created by users of an online system or service.

Virtual Gifts: Digital items that fans can purchase and send to creators as a form of support or appreciation.

Virtual Private Network (VPN): A service that encrypts your internet connection and hides your online identity.

Vibrator: A sex toy that uses vibration to provide sexual pleasure and stimulation, available in various shapes and intensities.

Viral Content: Content that quickly becomes very popular by being shared widely.

WeTransfer: An internet-based file transfer service company.

Whitelist: A list of approved entities, typically to receive certain privileges or services.

Wellness: The overall state of health, including physical, mental, and emotional aspects, achieved through proper self-care and lifestyle choices.

Whore: A derogatory term used to describe someone, usually a woman, who engages in sexual activity for money. It is a highly offensive and disrespectful term.

Workflow: The sequence of processes through which a piece of work passes from initiation to completion.

Zoom Show: A live, interactive video performance hosted on the Zoom platform, often used by adult entertainers to engage with their audience in real-time.

Support Services

- National Sexual Assault Hotline. (n.d.). Retrieved from National Sexual Assault Hotline website
- Adult Performers Actors Guild (APAG). (n.d.). Retrieved from APAG Union Resources for Mental Health

These sources provide additional information, support, and resources related to the topics discussed in this book.

Recommended Readings and Documentaries

- "The Truth Women Hate To Hear" (Self-Help Book)
- Lust, L. (n.d.). *The Performer's Guide to the Adult Industry*.
- "After Porn Ends" (Documentary Series). (n.d.).
- "Hot Girls Wanted" (Documentary). (n.d.).
- Lifting To Feel Lifted (Self-Help Book, Health Guide)

About the Author

Hey, I'm LaTre'. My journey's been anything but ordinary. I spent years making waves in the adult industry, racking up thousands of supporters and millions of views on Pornhub and Xvideos, while also landing in the top 14% of earners on OnlyFans. Now that I'm retired from that scene, I'm all about helping others navigate it smartly—making money and staying protected without the drama.

On top of that, I'm an international artist with a passion for music. I create melodic tracks that have connected with listeners around the globe, and I've accumulated over 300K streams across all platforms and still growing. If you are interested in hearing something just type in "Taylor MF'n Port" in a Google search. I should come right up.

Writing has been my thing for over 20 years. My arsenal is crazy and growing just like my music. Two books by me are "The Truth Women Hate To Hear," which keeps shit real and tells a harsh truth to women they tend to not accept, and "Slether:

The Origins of a Snake Man," a dive into some wild superhero fiction, Imagine Spider-Man mixed with The Boondocks.

I love crafting stories that let you escape from reality, but I'm even more into delivering those hard-hitting truths that bring you back to what's real. Through my music, writing, and industry insights, I'm all about blending creativity with raw honesty—giving you an escape when you need it and a reality check when it's time.

www.ingramcontent.com/pod-product-compliance
Lightning Source LLC
Chambersburg PA
CBHW050641160426
43194CB00010B/1763